The First Sin

JEWISH, CHRISTIAN, AND ISLAMIC PERSPECTIVES

First Edition
(1435 AH/2014 AC)

Copyright © 1435 AH/2014 AC
amana publications
10710 Tucker Street
Beltsville, MD 20705-2223 USA
Tel. 301.595.5777
Fax 301.595.5888, 240.250.3000
Email: amana@igprinting.com
        amana@amana-corp.com
Website: www.amana-publications.com

Library of Congress Cataloging-in-Publication Data

Dirks, Jerald.
  The first sin : Jewish, Christian, and Islamic perspectives / Jerald F. Dirks.
     pages cm.
  Includes bibliographical references.
  ISBN 978-1-59008-078-8
  1. Sin--Islam. 2. Sin--Judaism. 3. Sin--Christianity. 4. Pride and vanity. 5. Devil--Islam.
  6. Devil--Judaism. 7. Devil--Christianity. I. Title.
  BP166.75.D57 2014
  202'.2--dc23
                            2014006827

The First Sin

JEWISH, CHRISTIAN, AND ISLAMIC PERSPECTIVES

JERALD F. DIRKS

amana publications

All quotations of the English translation of the meaning of the *Qur'an* are taken from *The Meaning of the Holy Qur'an in Today's English—Extended Study Edition*, translated by Yahiya Emerick, copyright 2000, Islamic Foundation of North America, New York, New York. These quotations are used by permission of the author.

With regard to all Biblical quotations appearing in the text, unless specifically identified as being from another source, the following statement is noted in conformity with the request of the copyright holder.

"The Scripture quotations contained herein are from the *New Revised Standard Version Bible*, copyright 1989, by the Division of Christian Education of the National Council of the Churches of Christ in the U.S.A. Used by permission. All rights reserved."

Table of Contents

Acknowledgements vii

CHAPTER ONE
Introduction 1

CHAPTER TWO
The First Sin—Religious Texts 10

CHAPTER THREE
On Arrogance, Haughtiness, Pride, and Self-Conceit 44

CHAPTER FOUR
Arrogance in Race 80

CHAPTER FIVE
Arrogance in Religion 94

CHAPTER SIX
Spreading Sin 108

Bibliography 163

Acknowledgements

NO AUTHOR WRITES IN a vacuum, and all authors are at least somewhat beholden to those who have written before them. That is certainly true for me, and I am indebted to numerous prior authors, both living and dead, who have influenced my perspective and mindset far beyond my own conscious awareness of their influence. Likewise, I know that my thinking has been shaped throughout my life, at least in part, by numerous different teachers and professors, as well as by various Christian ministers, Jewish rabbis, and Muslim *Imams*. To all of the above, I owe a debt of gratitude. Without them, this book and the others that I have authored would not have been possible.

More specifically, there are numerous individuals who have directly contributed to making this book possible. To begin with, I want to thank Yahiya Emerick for his kind and generous permission to quote extensive passages from his recent translation of the *Qur'an* into modern American English. The present book is much enriched by being able to quote from his translation, the full citation for which is listed in the bibliography at the end of this book. Additionally, I wish to thank Rodd Umlauf for his assistance in researching early Christian beliefs about the first sin. His friendship and support have been a true example of interfaith communication. Likewise, I need to acknowledge the help and support of my publisher, Amana Publications, and its devoted staff of editors, graphic artists, and layout specialists. This is the eighth book of mine that Amana has published, and their encouragement and support have always been vital ingredients in motivating me to write. Finally, I cannot begin to thank my wife Debra enough for all her emotional support, her proofreading, and her willingness to pick up some of my other responsibilities so that I could have the time to write. For over 44 years of blissful married life, she has been my constant companion, the love of my life, and my most important helpmate among all of humanity.

Finally, I humbly thank God for giving me the opportunity to write this book. Whatever accuracy and insight there is to be found within this book's pages are due to Him. Whatever errors this book may contain are mine alone and should not in any way be attributed to those I have previously acknowledged as contributing to this book.

Jerald F. Dirks, M.Div., Psy.D.
September, 2013

Chapter One
Introduction

SETTING THE STAGE

THE THREE GREAT ABRAHAMIC faiths of Judaism, Christianity, and Islam have much that they hold in common. They share the same basic creation story, and all three religions are based on their acceptance of what they perceive to be divine revelation that was given to people by various prophets who spoke as God's instruments. The three religions even share much of the same prophetic history, including such stories as: (1) Adam's creation and fall; (2) Noah and the flood; (3) Abraham and Sarah in Egypt, Abraham taking Hagar as a second wife and fathering Ishmael, and Abraham's intended sacrifice of his son; (4) Isaac being born late in the lives of his parents, Abraham and Sarah; (5) Jacob, the son of Isaac; (6) Joseph, the son of Jacob, and his ability to interpret dreams, being sold into captivity in Egypt, and later rising to a position of great prominence in the Egyptian government; (7) Moses being cast onto the waters as an infant, being adopted by the pharaoh's family, killing an Egyptian as an adult and fleeing to Midian, and Moses and Aaron later leading the Israelites out of Egypt; (8) Samuel selecting Saul to be the first king of Israel; (9) David slaying Goliath; (10) Solomon and his wisdom; (11) Elijah; (12) Elisha; (13) Job being tried with numerous afflictions and yet remaining patient and steadfast in his faith; and (14) Jonah being swallowed by a whale or great fish.[1] Finally, the three Abrahamic faiths share many, if not most, of the same ethical and religious teachings.[2]

---

[1] For an in-depth discussion of the common ground in prophetic history that is shared by Judaism, Christianity, and Islam, see chapter two of Dirks JF (2003) and chapter three of Dirks JF (2004).
[2] For a fuller listing of the shared ethical and spiritual teachings to be found among Judaism, Christianity, and Islam, see chapter three of Dirks JF (2004).

THE FIRST SIN: JEWISH, CHRISTIAN, AND ISLAMIC PERSPECTIVES

Unfortunately, the adherents of Judaism, Christianity, and Islam frequently fail to recognize and celebrate this enormous common ground. All too often, their adherents turn a blind eye to their shared prophetic history and to their mutually held ethical and religious teachings. Too frequently, they want to focus on and argue about their differences in dogma and doctrine, rather than acknowledge their shared taproot of divine revelation. In this regard, one often overlooked area of commonality among the Abrahamic faiths concerns the first recorded sin in the cosmos.

This first sin, i.e., Satan refusing to bow down to Adam when given a divine command to do so, is frequently and quite prominently mentioned in Islam's *Qur'an*, and it is also recorded in one of the Jewish books of the Old Testament Pseudepigrapha. While Christian scripture does not mention this first sin, the religious writings of all three Abrahamic faiths are quite explicit in condemning the arrogance, pride, haughtiness, and self-conceit that resided behind Satan's refusal to obey God.

A WORD ABOUT SOURCES

INTRODUCTION

There is a voluminous literature for each of the three Abrahamic faiths, and it would be impossible to wade through all of this written material in a quest to winnow out everything that has been written that may touch upon the topic of the first sin. Furthermore, it would not be desirable to include all of this literature, as the texts in question vary greatly as to their perceived authority within their respective religious traditions. As such, before beginning our quest, it is first necessary to create a yardstick or hierarchy with regard to the literature of each of the three Abrahamic faiths and to establish some basic rules with regard to when and how the various literatures will be used.

THE JEWISH LITERATURE

At the top of the hierarchy of Jewish religious literature is the *Tanakh*,

INTRODUCTION

Judaism's official book of scripture. The *Tanakh* is comprised of three component parts: the Torah (the law or teachings,[3] the Nevi'im (the prophets),[4] and the Ketuvim (the writings).[5] Although there are some differences between the *Tanakh* and the Protestant Old Testament in terms of the names of individual Old Testament books, the order in which those books are arranged, and how those books are divided,[6] the *Tanakh* otherwise corresponds to the Protestant Old Testament. The *Tanakh* will hereinafter simply be referred to as the Old Testament, and all of the following quotations from and references to the Old Testament are from the New Revised Standard Version of the Old Testament. In presenting the Jewish literature on the first sin, the Old Testament will always be given precedence over any other Jewish literature.

While the Old Testament is the primary religious authority for Judaism, Orthodox Judaism maintains that it is only through the *Talmud* that the Old Testament may be properly interpreted and understood. Thus, for Orthodox Jews, although not necessarily for Reform Jews, the *Talmud* is second in religious authority only to the Old Testament. Comprised of two parts, i.e., the Mishnah and the Gemara, there are two versions of the *Talmud*, i.e., the Jerusalem version and the Babylonian version. The two versions share the same Mishnah, which was completed early in the third century CE, but have differing Gemaras, with the Babylonian version, which was completed around the start of the sixth

---

[3] The Torah conforms to Genesis, Exodus, Leviticus, Numbers, and Deuteronomy in the Protestant Old Testament.
[4] The Nevi'im conforms to Joshua, Judges, I & II Samuel, I & II Kings, Isaiah, Jeremiah, Ezekiel, Hosea, Joel, Amos, Obadiah, Jonah, Micah, Nahum, Habakkuk, Zephaniah, Haggai, Zechariah, and Malachi in the Protestant Old Testament.
[5] The Ketuvim conforms to Psalms, Proverbs, Job, Song of Solomon, Ruth, Lamentations, Ecclesiastes, Esther, Daniel, Ezra, Nehemiah, and I & II Chronicles in the Protestant Old Testament.
[6] For a fuller discussion of these differences between the *Tanakh* and the Protestant Old Testament, see chapter one of Dirks JF (2011).

century CE, being larger and usually considered to be more authoritative than the Jerusalem version, which was completed around the start of the fifth century CE. Given the above, the *Babylonian Talmud* earns a strong second place in our hierarchy of Jewish literature and will be utilized whenever possible in considering the Jewish perspective on the first sin. In what follows, no distinction will be made between the Mishnah and the Gemara when quoting from the *Babylonian Talmud*.[7]

In reporting the first known sin, neither the Old Testament nor the *Babylonian Talmud* presents the needed information or presents only part of the Jewish perspective. As such, use is made of a third category of Jewish literature, which is comprised of the Old Testament Apocrypha and the Old Testament Pseudepigrapha, each of which is comprised of numerous books that were written between approximately 300 BCE and 100 CE. Whenever any material is initially used from one of these books, the reader will be provided with relevant information about the book in question, including what is known about the date of composition, authorship, etc. This additional information may be included either in the text of this book itself or in a footnote. Finally, it should be noted that all quotations from the Old Testament Apocrypha are taken from the New Revised Standard Version of the Bible.

THE CHRISTIAN LITERATURE

For Christians, the literature of primary religious authority is the *Bible*. However, the various denominations of Christendom have never totally agreed as to which books constitute either the Old Testament or the New Testament.[8] As such, some definition is needed as to what will be

---

[7] For a fuller discussion of the Mishnah, Gemara, *Palestinian Talmud*, and *Babylonian Talmud*, see chapter six of Dirks JF (2011).

[8] For a fuller discussion of the differing Old and New Testaments that are recognized by different Christian denominations, see chapter one of Dirks JF (2011).

Introduction

considered the *Bible* in the present work. Briefly stated, the *Bible* will be considered to consist of: the 39-book Protestant Old Testament, plus the 27-book New Testament that is jointly recognized by the Protestant, Roman Catholic, Greek Orthodox, and Russian Orthodox churches. In what follows, all New Testament quotations are taken from the New Revised Standard Version of the *Bible*.

While the *Bible* as defined above will be considered the primary religious text of Christianity, secondary status will then be given to the various books of the Old Testament Apocrypha, which are recognized as part of the Old Testament by adherents of the Roman Catholic, Greek Orthodox, and Russian Orthodox traditions. Finally, tertiary status will be given to the writings of the early Church Fathers.

The Islamic Literature

The *Qur'an* is the sacred scripture recognized by Islam. Muslims believe that the *Qur'an* contains the actual words of God as revealed to Prophet Muhammad by the angel Gabriel, with such revelation beginning in the year 610 CE, and with subsequent passages of the *Qur'an* being sporadically revealed over the course of the next 22 years. In its completed form, the *Qur'an* consists of 114 chapters (*Surat* in the plural form of Arabic and *Surah* in the singular form), ranging in size from a low of three (*Surah Al-Kawthar*) to a high of 286 (*Surah Al-Baqarah*) verses. Both Sunni and Shia Muslims recognize the *Qur'an* to be the highest religious authority within Islam. As such, the *Qur'an* is herein given prominence over all other Islamic sources.[9] In what follows, all quotations from the *Qur'an* are taken from Yahiya Emerick's recent translation of the *Qur'an* into modern American English.

---

[9] For a fuller discussion of the provenance, language, and form and structure of the *Qur'an*, see chapter four of Dirks JF (2003).

The Arabic word "*Sunnah*" literally means a well-trodden path, but it can also refer to the customary practice of a person or group. Within an Islamic context, the *Sunnah* refers to the religious teachings and customary religious practice of Prophet Muhammad. With regard to the *Sunnah*, the *Qur'an* repeatedly proclaims that Muslims are to obey Prophet Muhammad and to follow his illustrious example of behavior and conduct.[10] As such, the *Sunnah* of Prophet Muhammad is religiously authoritative and binding on all Muslims.

The *Sunnah* of Prophet Muhammad is encapsulated within the *Ahadith* (singular = *Hadith*), which are narrations in which other people stated what Prophet Muhammad reportedly said and did with regard to the religion of Islam. Unfortunately, some of these narrations have less than absolute authenticity, which has prompted Muslim scholars of the past to do elaborate and in-depth research into the provenance of these *Ahadith*. After much painstaking research into the provenance and authenticity of these *Ahadith*, Sunni Muslims typically recognize six multi-volume collections of *Ahadith* to be the most authentic and authoritative. These are the collections of (1) Al-Bukhari (Abu 'Abd Allah Muhammad ibn Isma'il ibn Ibrahim Al-Bukhari Al-Jufi'), who lived from 810 to 870 CE, and whose collection is *Kitab Al-Jami' Al-Sahih* (referenced herein as *Bukhari*) and contains approximately 7,000 narrations, some of which are repeated; (2) Muslim (Abu Al-Husain 'Asakir Al-Din Muslim ibn Al-Hajjaj Al-Qushayri Al-Naisabori), who lived from approximately 820 to 875 CE, and whose collection is known as *Al-Jami' Al-Sahih* (referenced herein as *Muslim*) and contains about 7,000 narrations, some of which are repeated; (3) Abu Dawud (Abu Dawud Sulayman ibn Al-Ashath Al-Azdi Al-Sijistani), who lived from circa 818 to 889 CE, and whose collection is known

---

[10] See, for example, *Qur'an* 3:132; 4:42, 59, 64-65, 80, 115; 5:92; 7:157-158; 33:21; and 48:10.

INTRODUCTION

as *Kitab Al-Sunan* (referenced herein as *Abu Dawud*) and contains over 5,000 narrations; (4) Al-Tirmidhi (Abu 'Isa Muhammad ibn 'Isa ibn Sawrah ibn Shaddad Al-Tirmidhi), who lived from 824 to 892 CE, and whose collection is known variously as *Al-Jami' Al-Kabir, Al-Jami' Al-Sahih,* and *Sunan Al-Tirmidhi* (referenced herein as *Tirmidhi*) and contains almost 4,000 narrations; (5) Nasa'i (Abu 'Abd Al-Rahman Ahmad ibn Shu'ayb ibn 'Ali Al-Khursani Al-Nasa'i), who lived from about 830 to 916 CE, and whose collection is known variously as *Al-Sunan Al-Mujtaba* and *Al-Sunan Al-Nasa'i;* and (6) Ibn Majah (Abu 'Abd Allah Muhammad Yazeed Al-Rabi Al-Qazwini), who lived from 824 to 886 CE, and whose collection includes 4,341 narrations, approximately 613 of which are considered to be of weak provenance and 99 of which are believed to have been fabricated). The first four of these collections of *Ahadith* are used with some frequency in the present work and will be considered secondary only to the *Qur'an* in the hierarchy of Islamic authority. Other collections of *Ahadith* that may be cited in this book include those of: (1) Ahmad ibn Hanbal, who lived from 780 to 855 CE, and whose collection is known as the *Musnad* (referenced herein as *Ahmad*); and (2) Imam Malik (Abu 'Abdullah Malik ibn Anas ibn Al-Harith Al-Asbahi), who lived from circa 715 to 795 CE, and whose collection is known as *Al-Muwatta* (referenced herein as *Malik*). Occasionally, use will be made of some additional sources of *Ahadith*.[11]

Occasionally, a third category of Islamic literature will be used within

---

[11] For a fuller discussion of the *Sunnah* of Prophet Muhammad and of the history and provenance of the *Ahadith* collections of Sunni Islam, see chapter four of Dirks JF (2003). Shia Muslims have their own collections of *Ahadith*, e.g., *Al-Kafi* of Imam Ja'far Al-Sadiq and *Nahjul Balagha* of Imam 'Ali ibn Abu Talib. In contrast to the Sunni *Ahadith* that trace back to Prophet Muhammad, the Shia collections typically record the statements of their recognized Imams, i.e., 'Ali ibn Abu Talib or one of the descendants of Prophet Muhammad who are recognized by the Shia as being their religious leaders. Depending upon the Shia sect in question, five, seven, or 12 different Imams are recognized.

the pages of this book. This third category consists of commentaries on the *Qur'an*, as well as Islamic tradition that may trace back to a companion of Prophet Muhammad, but not back to Prophet Muhammad himself. Such instances will always be identified, and the background material on that source will always be provided the first time that source is utilized.

PREVIEWING THE CHAPTERS

As noted previously, the first recorded sin is that of Satan's refusal to obey the divine command to bow down to Adam. This first sin is recounted numerous times in the *Qur'an* and at least once in the Old Testament Pseudepigrapha. Chapter two presents the religious texts of Islam and Judaism that deal with the first sin and with Satan's subsequent fall from grace. These texts are quoted verbatim, and their references are given. The Islamic and Jewish texts are then compared and contrasted. As will be seen, both the Islamic and Jewish texts maintain that Satan's initial sin grew out of the character flaws of arrogance, haughtiness, pride, and self-conceit. However, there are several significant differences that emerge between the Islamic texts and the Jewish text, including Satan's name and category of being, whether or not racism is part and parcel of Satan's arrogance, whether or not Satan actually sees himself as potentially God's equal, and the issue of Adam being allegedly created in the image of God. The chapter then ends with a brief consideration of the narcissistic personality, a psychological construct that appears to fit rather nicely with the Islamic texts' portrayal of Satan.

Given that arrogance lies at the very heart of the first sin, chapter three focuses on Jewish, Christian, and Islamic religious texts that address and condemn such personality traits as arrogance, haughtiness, pride, and self-conceit, as well as those that praise humility, which is the opposite of arrogance. Chapters four and five continue the initial discussion on the

INTRODUCTION

general topic of arrogance by looking at two specific forms of arrogance: (1) racism and ethnic bigotry, which are nothing more or less than an overwhelming arrogance in one's race or ethnic heritage; and (2) arrogance in religious practice.

Chapter six picks up on Satan's vindictive boast, found in some of the Islamic accounts of the first sin, that he will spread sin and transgression among mankind and will lead many men and women astray. This Satanic threat may be seen as part and parcel of Satan's sin of arrogance and of his own refusal to accept self-responsibility for his initial transgression. As such, chapter six tours the pages of history through the lenses of the *Bible*, the *Babylonian Talmud*, the Old Testament Apocrypha, and the *Qur'an* to look at examples of Satan's success in spreading the sin of arrogance among mankind.

Chapter Two
The First Sin–Religious Texts

ISLAMIC TEXTS

INTRODUCTION

THE STORY OF THE FIRST known sin in the universe is told seven different times in the *Qur'an*. Some of these passages are rather short and to the point, while others are considerably longer and offer a wealth of detail and context. The very fact that the story of the first sin appears so frequently within the pages of the *Qur'an* suggests that there is much that one should learn from this first recorded sin and that it offers a blueprint for failure that mankind should avoid at all costs.

THE QUR'ANIC ACCOUNTS

In the two shortest Qur'anic accounts of this first sin, the reader is basically told only that Satan refused the direct command of God to bow down to Adam, the first human. In these two passages, Satan is referred to as a jinn named Iblis who used to gather with the angels. Both the name "Iblis" and the creation known as the jinn are discussed in some detail later in this chapter when contrasting the Jewish and Islamic accounts of the first sin.

> We told the angels, "Bow down to Adam," and they all bowed down, except for Iblis, who was one of the jinns. He broke away from his Lord's command. (*Qur'an* 18:50, Emerick translation)

> When We said to the angels, "Bow down to Adam," they all bowed down. However, (a jinn named) Iblis didn't bow down, for he refused. (*Qur'an* 20:116, Emerick translation)

The First Sin–Religious Texts

Why did Satan refuse to obey his Lord? How could anyone stand before God, see His glory and grandeur with one's own eyes, hear His command in a direct and unmistakable way with one's own ears, and then basically thumb one's nose at God? How could it have happened? What was behind this first sin? What could have possibly motivated Satan to defy the Almighty? What was the rootstock from which this first sin grew?

The most primitive answer to each of the above questions is simply to maintain that the first sin was caused by defiance of and rebellion against God's decree—"He broke away from his Lord's command... he refused." However, such a response is much too overly generalized to give any real insight into the first sin. After all, isn't all sin somehow an act of defiance against one or another of God's commandments? A much more specific and pointed answer is delineated in the lengthier Qur'anic accounts of the first sin, and that answer involves the traits and attitudes variously known as pride, haughtiness, conceit, arrogance, bigotry, and racism.

> So then We gave an order to the angels, saying, "Bow down (in respect) to Adam." Then they all bowed down; however, (a jinn named) Iblis (who was there watching) didn't bow down. He refused in his arrogant pride and chose to suppress (his awareness of the truth). (*Qur'an* 2:34, Emerick translation)

> And so it was that We created you and gave you your shape. We then ordered the angels to bow down to (your original ancestor) Adam, and they all bowed down, except for (a jinn named) Iblis, who didn't bow at all! God said to him, "What's preventing you from bowing down, when I've commanded it?"

> "I'm better than he is," (Iblis) replied, "for You made me from fire, while You made him from clay."

The First Sin: Jewish, Christian, and Islamic Perspectives

"Get down and away from here!" (God) ordered. "This is no place for you to be arrogant. Get out of here, for you're the least (of all creatures)."

"Give me time!" (Iblis) cried out. "(Give me time) until the day when they're all resurrected."

"You shall have your time," (God) answered. Then Iblis said, "And since it was You Who made me slip up, I'll lie in wait for them on Your 'straight path.' I'll attack them from their front and their back and from their right and their left, and in the end You'll see that most of them are thankless (towards You)."

"Get out of here!" (God) ordered, "You're banished! If any of them follow you, then I'll fill Hellfire with you all!" (*Qur'an* 7:11-18, Emerick translation)

And so it was that We created human beings from pliable clay—from mere molded mud, and We created the jinns, even before (human beings), from the intense heat (of pure energy).

Your Lord said to the angels, "I'm going to create mortal man from mineral-rich clay, from molded mud. After I've constructed him and breathed into him (something of) My spirit, you must all prostrate to him (out of respect)."

The angels fell down in prostration all together, but Iblis didn't (join with the angels), for he refused to be with those who prostrated. Then God asked, "Iblis! What's wrong with you that you didn't join those who prostrated?"

"I'm not going to prostrate myself to a mortal man," Iblis answered, "for You created him from mineral-rich clay, from mere molded mud!"

"Then get out of here!" God ordered. "You're an outcast, and you'll be cursed all the way to the Day of Judgment!"

"My Lord!" Iblis cried out. "Give me some time until they're resurrected."

"You'll have your time," (God said), "until a day whose arrival is appointed."

"My Lord!" (Iblis) said. "Since You made me slip up, I'm going to make (immorality and wickedness) seem proper and good to those on earth, and I'm going to deviate all of them (morally)— except, (of course), for Your sincere servants among them."

"The path (that they follow) will be the straight one that leads back to Me," (God) answered, "and you'll have no power over My servants, except for the ones who put themselves in the wrong and follow you." Hellfire is the promised destination of them all! There will be seven gates (leading within it) – one gate for each class (of sinners). (*Qur'an* 15:26-44, Emerick translation)

When We told the angels, "Bow down (in respect) to Adam," they all bowed down. Iblis, however, (who was a jinn in their company, did not bow along with them).

"How can I bow down to a creature that You made from mud?" he asked. "Look at that!" he continued. "This (human) is the one whom You're honoring over me! If You give me a chance until the Day of Assembly, I'll make his descendants blindly obedient (to me), all but a few!"

"Go away," (God) replied, "and if any of them follow you, then Hellfire will be enough of a reward for you all! Mesmerize any of them that you can with your (alluring) voice (of temptation). Assail them with your cavalry and with your infantry. Share in their wealth and children, and make promises to them—even though the promises of Satan are nothing more than deception. As for My servants, however, you will have no power over them. Your Lord is quite enough to take care (of them)." (*Qur'an* 17: 61-65, Emerick translation)

Your Lord said to the angels, "I'm going to create mortal humans from clay. After I've formed him completely and then breathed into him of My spirit, you must all fall down prostrate before him." So all the angels fell down together in prostration, but (a jinn named) Iblis did not (join in), for he became proud and lost his faith.

(God) asked him, "Iblis! Why haven't you prostrated yourself to a being that I've created with My Own hands? Are you too proud, or are you so high and mighty?"

"I'm better than him," (Iblis) answered. "You made me from fire, while You made him from clay."

"Get out of here," (God) commanded, "for you shall be an outcast! My curse will mark you until the Day of Judgment!"

"My Lord!" (Iblis) cried. "Give me time until the day You resurrect (them)."

"You shall have your time," (God) replied, "until the day the scheduled event comes to pass."

"Then," Iblis said, "by the token of Your Own Power, know that I'm going to seduce them all, except for Your sincere servants, of course."

"Then that's the truth of it, and what I say is true," (God) declared. "I will fill Hellfire with you and all who follow you, all together." (*Qur'an* 38:71-85, Emerick translation)

"He refused in his arrogant pride... I'm better than he is... he became proud and lost his faith... Are you too proud, or are you so high and mighty?" Pride, haughtiness, conceit, and arrogance—here is the taproot from which grows the first known sin. Here is the rootstock from which all too easily grows the bitter plant of bigotry and racism. Just listen to the arrogant racism implicit in the words of Satan. "'I'm better than he is,' (Iblis) replied, 'for You made me from fire, while You made him from clay... I'm not going to prostrate myself to a mortal man,' Iblis answered, 'for You created him from mineral-rich clay, from mere molded mud... How can I bow down to a creature that You made from mud... I'm better than him,' (Iblis) answered. 'You made me from fire, while You made him from clay.'" I'm better than he is; I was made from a superior substance than the one from which he was made; I am constitutionally superior to him. Therein is the arrogant bigotry and racism underlying Satan's first sin.

In considering the above passages from the *Qur'an*, it is instructive to focus on *Qur'an* 7:12, 15:33, 17:61, and 38:76. All four verses give some insight into Satan's arrogance, in that these verses document the first time that a mere entity from God's creation uses the first person singular pronoun, i.e., "I." It is Satan's focus on himself rather than on God that underlies his arrogance. It is Satan's infatuation with "I" and "me" that is part and parcel of the first sin.

JEWISH TEXTS

INTRODUCTION

The story of the first sin appears neither in the Old Testament nor in the *Babylonian Talmud*. However, it does appear in the Life of Adam and

Eve, which is part of the Old Testament Pseudepigrapha, and the story of God commanding the angels to bow down to Adam may also be found in the Jewish Midrashic literature.[12] As the Life of Adam and Eve is likely to be unfamiliar to most readers, a brief digression is in order to provide some background on this book.

Existing texts for the Life of Adam and Eve are to be found in Greek, Latin, Slavic, and Armenian, and they variously date from the ninth through 17th centuries. However, it is most likely that the Life of Adam and Eve was originally written in Hebrew or Aramaic and that the Hebrew or Aramaic original was then translated into Greek by at least 400 CE. While it is possible the first Latin translation was made directly from the Semitic original, it is more likely that it, like the Slavic and Armenian texts, was a translation from the Greek translation. As to when the Semitic original was first written, the broader answer would be sometime between 100 BCE and 200 CE, and the narrower answer would be in the first century CE. The original author of the Life of Adam and Eve remains unknown, but the internal evidence from the book would suggest that he was a Jew of Pharisaic persuasion who was most likely living in Palestine. As to the book's classification in terms of type of writing, it should probably be considered a Midrash or Haggadah not unlike those found among the Dead Sea Scrolls and writings of the rabbis of Pharisaic Judaism.[13]

---

[12] The Midrashic account reads as follows. "(How did) Adam the protoplast (do so)? The day when he was endowed with his knowledge, the Holy One, blessed be He, commanded the ministering angels: 'Enter and bow down to him!' The ministering angels entered to perform the will of the Holy One, blessed be He. (However,) Satan, who was the mightiest of all the angels in heaven, said to the Holy One, blessed be He, 'Master of the universe! You created us from the Divine Glory, and now You say to us, 'Bow yourselves down!' before one whom You created from the dirt of the earth??!?' The Holy One, blessed be He, answered him: 'This one who originates (from) the dirt of the earth possesses some wisdom and intelligence which is not in you!'" (Albeck H, 1940)

[13] Johnson MD (2011).

The Life of Adam and Eve

The text quoted below recounts a conversation between Adam and Satan that is preserved only in the Latin text of the Life of Adam and Eve. The conversation supposedly takes place after Adam's and Eve's partaking of the forbidden fruit and their later expulsion from the Garden of Eden. The conversation begins with Satan starting to explain why he strives to deceive the first two humans and why he continues to tempt them into sinning.

And the devil sighed and said, "O Adam, all my enmity and envy and sorrow concern you, since because of you I am expelled and deprived of my glory which I had in the heavens in the midst of angels, and because of you I was cast out onto the earth."

Adam answered, "What have I done to you, and what is my blame with you? Since you are neither harmed nor hurt by us, why do you pursue us?"

The devil replied, "Adam, what are you telling me? It is because of you that I have been thrown out of there. When you were created, I was cast out from the presence of God and was sent out from the fellowship of angels. When God blew into you the breath of life and your countenance and likeness were made in the image of God, Michael brought you and made (us) worship you in the sight of God, and the Lord God said, 'Behold Adam! I have made you in our image and likeness.' And Michael went out and called all the angels, saying, 'Worship the image of the Lord God, as the Lord God has instructed.' And Michael himself worshiped first, and called me and said, 'Worship the image of God, Yahweh.' And I answered, 'I do not worship Adam.' And when Michael kept forcing me to worship, I said to him, 'Why do you compel me? I will not worship one inferior and subsequent to me. I am prior to him in creation; before he was made, I was already made. He ought to worship me.' When they heard this, other angels who were under me refused to worship him. And Michael asserted, 'Worship the image of God. But if now you will not worship, the Lord God will be wrathful with you.' And I said, 'If he be wrathful with me, I will set my throne above the stars of heaven and will be like the Most High.' And the Lord God was angry with me and sent me with my angels out from our glory; and because of you, we were expelled into this world from our dwellings and have been cast onto the earth. And immediately we were made to grieve, since we had been deprived of so great glory. And we were pained to see you in such bliss of delights. So with deceit I assailed your wife and made you to be expelled through her from the joys of your bliss, as I have been expelled from my glory." (Life of Adam and Eve 12:1-16:3)[14]

COMPARING AND CONTRASTING THE ISLAMIC AND JEWISH TRADITIONS

Iblis Vs. Satan

In the Life of Adam and Eve, Satan is referred to merely as the devil, although it may be assumed by context that this devil is Satan. Satan is etymologically derived from the three-letter Hebrew root word *s-t-n*, which means adversary.[15] Within the pages of the Old Testament, Satan is variously referred to as the serpent (Genesis 3:1-15),[16] Satan (I Chronicles 21:1), Azazel (Leviticus 16:8-10 & 26, where it is sometimes translated as scapegoat etc.), and Lucifer or the "Day Star" (Isaiah 14:12). Within some

---
[14] Johnson MD (2011), page 262.
[15] (A) Kuemmerlin-McLean J (1997); (B) Smith W (---).
[16] Later Jewish writing sometimes makes the distinction that Satan was not the serpent, but that Satan used the serpent as his instrument.

of the Dead Sea Scrolls, the Old Testament Apocrypha, and the Old Testament Pseudepigrapha, Satan is also known as Mastema, Beliar, Asmodeus, and Sammael.[17]

Twice in Tobit, one of the books of the Old Testament Apocrypha, reference is made to Asmodeus, a wicked demon who appears to be Satan.[18] (Tobit is a book of historical fiction, whose setting is the eighth century BCE.[19] Despite this setting, Biblical scholars are in agreement that the book was written much later than its setting. Some scholars suggest that Tobit was originally composed in Aramaic by a Jew living in Egypt late in the third century BCE.[20] Other scholars suggest a date ranging from the mid fourth century BCE to early in the second century BCE, a Jewish author living in Syria or Mesopotamia, and a language of composition that could have been either Hebrew, Aramaic, or Greek.[21]) The relevant verses from Tobit are quoted immediately below.

> For she had been married to seven husbands, and the wicked demon Asmodeus had killed each of them before they had been with her as is customary for wives…So Raphael was sent to heal both of them: Tobit, by removing the white films from his eyes, so that he might see God's light with his eyes; and Sarah, daughter of Raguel, by giving her in marriage to Tobias son of Tobit, and by setting her free from the wicked demon Asmodeus. (Tobit 3:8 & 17, NRSV)

With regard to Satan being known by the name Mastema, one only has to consider the book of Jubilees, one of the books of the Old Testament Pseudepigrapha, where Satan is portrayed as being the instigator behind the trial of Abraham being asked to sacrifice his son. (Jubilees, a.k.a. The

---
[17] (A) Vinson RB (1997); (B) Jacobs J, Blau L (---); (C) Knibb MA (2011).
[18] Jacobs J, Blau L (---).
[19] Peacock HF (1997a).
[20] Simpson DC (1971).
[21] (A) Peacock HF (1997a); (B) Richardson HN (1971a).

Little Genesis, was originally written no later than the second century BCE in Hebrew by an anonymous Jew who was living in Palestine and who appears to have been a member of the Hasidic or pre-Essenic sect of Judaism. The Hebrew original of Jubilees was subsequently translated into Greek and Syriac, and the Greek translation was later translated into Latin and Ethiopic.[22]) The relevant passage from Jubilees immediately follows.

> And Prince Mastema came and he said before God, "Behold, Abraham loves Isaac, his son. And he is more pleased with him than everything. Tell him to offer him (as) a burnt offering upon the altar. And you will see whether he will do this thing. And you will know whether he is faithful in everything in which you test him." (Jubilees 17:16)[23]

Numerous examples exist with regard to Satan being known throughout several books of the Old Testament Pseudepigrapha by the name Beliar/Belial. Such references exist within the pages of Jubilees, the Ascension of Isaiah the Prophet,[24] the Testament of Levi,[25] and the

---

[22] Wintermute OS (2011).

[23] Wintermute OS (2011), page 90.

[24] The first part of the Ascension of Isaiah, i.e., the Martyrdom of Isaiah, was originally written in Hebrew by an anonymous Jew living in Palestine, probably during the second century BCE. Chapters 3:13-4:22 may be dated to the end of the first century CE, while later chapters are best dated from the second century CE to as late as the fourth century CE. Unfortunately, numerous Christian interpolations have been inserted into the text at various places. As such, it is not always clear whether a given passage represents Jewish or Christian thinking. Knibb MA (2011).

[25] The Testament of Levi is part of the Testaments of the Twelve Patriarchs, which was originally written in Greek by an anonymous, Hellenized Jew who was probably living in Syria during the second century BCE. Because some passages of the Testaments of the Twelve Patriarchs predict that two messiahs are to come, i.e., a priestly messiah from the tribe of Levi and a kingly messiah from the tribe of Judah, and because this same messianic concept occurs in some of the Dead Sea Scrolls, a link to the Essenic sect of Judaism can be posited. While the Testaments of the Twelve Patriarchs can be comfortably assigned to the second century BCE, the reader is advised that there are about 10-12 much later Christian interpolations into the text. Kee HC (2011).

Testament of Dan.[26] Some of the relevant passages from these books of the Old Testament Pseudepigrapha are quoted below.

> O Lord, let your mercy be lifted up upon your people, and create for them an upright spirit. And do not let the spirit of Beliar rule over them to accuse them before you and ensnare them from every path of righteousness so that they might be destroyed from before your face. (Jubilees 1:20)[27]

> ...and he will be a follower of Beliar rather than of me. He will cause many in Jerusalem and Judah to desert the true faith, and Beliar will dwell in Manasseh, and by his hands I will be sawed in half. (Ascension of Isaiah the Prophet 1:8-9)[28]

> In the second are the armies arrayed for the day of judgment to work vengeance on the spirits of error and of Beliar...And Beliar shall be bound by him (the priestly messiah)...And now, my children, you have heard everything. Choose for yourselves light or darkness, the Law of the Lord or the works of Beliar. (Testament of Levi 3:3; 18:12; 19:1)[29]

> Observe the Lord's commandments, then, my children, and keep his Law. Avoid wrath, and hate lying, in order that the Lord may dwell among you, and Beliar may flee from you...And there shall arise for you from the tribe of Judah and (the tribe of) Levi the Lord's salvation. He will make war against Beliar; he will grant the vengeance of victory as our goal. And he shall take from Beliar the captives, the souls of the saints...(Testament of Dan 5:1 & 10)[30]

---

[26] The Testament of Dan is part of the Testaments of the Twelve Patriarchs; see immediately preceding footnote for more details.
[27] Wintermute OS (2011), page 53.
[28] Knibb MA (2011), page 157.
[29] Kee HC (2011), pages 789 & 795.
[30] Kee HC (2011), page 809.

Finally, one finds Satan being known by the name Sammael/Samael in the *Palestinian Talmud* (Gen. R. 19)[31] and in the Ascension of Isaiah the Prophet. In fact, in the Old Testament Pseudepigrapha's Ascension of Isaiah the Prophet, the identification of Satan with Sammael is made explicit in that he is called Sammael Satan in 11:41.

> And Sammael Malkira[32] will serve Manasseh and will do everything he wishes...and Sammael dwelt in Manasseh and clung closely to him...And we went up into the firmament, I and he, and there I saw Sammael[33] and his hosts; and there was a great struggle in it, and the words of Satan, and they were envying one another...Because of these visions and prophecies Sammael Satan sawed Isaiah the son of Amoz, the prophet, in half by the hand of Manasseh. (Ascension of Isaiah the Prophet 1:8; 2:1; 7:9; 11:41)[34]

As the Old Testament is also Christian scripture, and as the Old Testament Apocrypha is accepted as Christian scripture by the Roman Catholic, Greek Orthodox, and Russian Orthodox churches and as Christian literature by the Protestant churches, many of the aforementioned names for Satan are also part and parcel of the Christian tradition. Additionally, within the pages of the Christian New Testament, Satan is variously known as the devil (e.g., Matthew 4:1; Luke 4:2; John 8:44; Revelation 12:7, 9, & 12, and 20:2 & 10), Satan (e.g., Matthew 12:26; Mark 3:23-26; Luke 11:18; Revelation 12:9 & 20:2 & 7), Beelzebul (e.g., Matthew 12:24-27; Mark 3:22; Luke 11:15-19), the evil one (e.g., Matthew 13:19), Beliar (II Corinthians 6:15), father of lies (John 8:44), and the dragon (e.g., Revelation 12: 7-9, 13-18, and 20:2).

While the Life of Adam and Eve refers to Satan as the devil, and while

---

[31] T Jacob J, Blau L (---).
[32] Malkira is Hebrew and may be translated as King of Evil, which is another name given to Satan. Knibb MA (2011).
[33] In some Latin, Slavonic, and Greek texts, the name Sammael is actually replaced with the name Satan. Knibb MA (2011).
[34] Knibb MA (2011), pages 157, 166, and 176.

the Old Testament, the Old Testament Apocrypha, the Old Testament Pseudepigrapha, and the Christian New Testament refer to Satan by a variety of names, the Qur'anic accounts quoted above refer to Satan as Iblis. The name Iblis occurs in eleven different Qur'anic verses, including 2:34, 7:11, 15:31-32, 17:61, 18:50, 20:116, 26:95, 34:20, and 38:74-75. In all of them, it is clear by context that Iblis is Satan.

Over time, different etymologies have been offered regarding the name Iblis. Algar[36] rather imaginatively seeks to derive it from the Greek word for accuser or devil, i.e., *diabolos*, but that appears to be quite a stretch. Far more likely is the derivation offered in Ibn Kathir's (Al-Hafiz Abu Al-Fida' 'Imad Ad-Din Ismail ibn 'Umar ibn Kathir Al-Qurashi Al-Busrawi, born in 1300 or 1301 CE in Busra and died between 1371 and 1373 CE in Damascus) monumental Arabic commentary on the *Qur'an*, which is typically considered to be one of the most authoritative commentaries on the *Qur'an*. Ibn Kathir maintained that the name derives from the Arabic word for despaired, i.e., *Ablasa* from the verbal root *b-l-s*, as in *Ablasa Min Ar-Rahmah*, i.e., despaired of mercy, for there was no hope for Satan to receive God's mercy after Satan's involvement in and the aftermath from the first sin.[37] Emerick appears to follow this same derivation in suggesting that Iblis derives from the Arabic word for frustrated and that Iblis' name was subsequently changed to Satan (*Shaytan*, i.e., to separate from), indicating that Satan was separated from God's fellowship and that Satan then sought to separate mankind from God's fellowship as well.[38] 'Abdullah Yusuf 'Ali appears to agree with this derivation, claiming that the name Iblis means desperateness or rebellion and that the name Satan implies perversity or enmity.[39]

---

[35] (A) Rutledge DW (1997); (B) Vinson RB (1997); (C) Sweet LM (2001).
[36] Algar H (1997).
[37] Ibn Kathir I (2000), volume 8, page 352, in his commentary on *Qur'an* 38:74-85.
[38] Emerick Y (2000), page 50, footnote 58, in his commentary on *Qur'an* 2:34.
[39] 'Ali 'A (2009), page 25, footnote 52, in his commentary on *Qur'an* 2:36.

As a side note to this whole issue of names, Ibn Kathir wrote that Muhammad ibn Ishaq claimed that Ibn 'Abbas[40] said that before he was called Iblis, Satan was known as Azazil.[41] However, in his monumental history of the world, *Tarikh Al-Rusul Wa Al-Muluk* (History of Messengers and Kings), Al-Tabari quotes Ibn 'Abbas as maintaining that Satan's original name was Al-Harith.[42] Which of the Ibn 'Abbas reports is accurate, if either, is in many ways immaterial to the Islamic perspective, as neither report represents the *Qur'an* or the *Sunnah* of Prophet Muhammad.

Jinn Vs. Fallen Angel

A significant difference between the Qur'anic accounts and The Life of Adam and Eve is that the latter source portrays Satan, at least by implication, as being a fallen angel, and it also states that other angels followed Satan's example. "When they heard this, other angels who were under me refused to worship him." No passage from the Old Testament explicitly refers to Satan as being a fallen angel, although the following passages, the first of which described an alleged event well after the fall of Satan, are often used as scriptural bases for positing the existence of fallen angels and for Satan being one of them.

> When people began to multiply on the face of the ground, and daughters were born to them, the sons of God saw that they were fair; and they took wives for themselves of all that they chose. Then the Lord said, "My spirit shall not abide in mortals forever,

---

[40] Ibn 'Abbas, a.k.a. 'Abd Allah ibn Al-'Abbas ibn 'Abdul Muttalib, was a first cousin of Prophet Muhammad. He was born circa 619, died circa 687 in Ta'if, and is credited with narrating some 1,660 *Ahadith*.

[41] Ibn Kathir I (2000), volume 1, page 194, in his commentary on *Qur'an* 2:34.

[42] Al-Tabari M (1989), page 252. Abu Ja'far Muhammad ibn Jarir Al-Tabari was born circa 839 in Amol, Tabaristan (Iran), and died in 923 in Baghdad, Iraq. He is best known for his Qur'anic commentary and for his world history. It is the latter of which that is referenced here.

for they are flesh; their days shall be one hundred twenty years." The Nephilim were on the earth in those days—and also afterward—when the sons of God went in to the daughters of humans, who bore children to them. These were the heroes that were of old, warriors of renown. (Genesis 6:1-4, NRSV)

How you are fallen from heaven, O Day Star,[43] son of Dawn! How you are cut down to the ground, you who laid the nations low! You said in your heart, "I will raise my throne above the stars of God; I will sit on the mount of assembly on the heights of Zaphon; I will ascend to the tops of the clouds, I will make myself like the Most High." But you are brought down to Sheol, to the depths of the Pit. (Isaiah 14:12-15, NRSV)

You were the signet of perfection, full of wisdom and perfect in beauty. You were in Eden, the garden of God; every precious stone was your covering, carnelian, chrysolite, and moonstone, beryl, onyx, and jasper, sapphire, turquoise, and emerald; and worked in gold were your settings and your engravings. On the day that you were created they were prepared. With an anointed cherub as guardian I placed you; you were on the holy mountain of God; you walked among the stones of fire. You were blameless in your ways from the day that you were created, until iniquity was found in you. In the abundance of your trade you were filled with violence, and you sinned; so I cast you as a profane thing from the mountain of God, and the guardian cherub drove you out from among the stones of fire. Your heart was proud because of your

---

[43] The Hebrew word that is translated as Day Star in the NRSV is *helel*, and the Day Star refers to the planet Venus. The Latin word for the planet Venus is Lucifer, which can also mean lightbearer, and it is from the Latin that Lucifer emerges as an alternate name for Satan. In the King James Version of the Bible, *helel* is translated as Lucifer, and the identification of the Day Star with Satan is complete.

beauty; you corrupted your wisdom for the sake of your splendor. I cast you to the ground; I exposed you before kings, to feast their eyes on you. By the multitude of your iniquities, in the unrighteousness of your trade, you profaned your sanctuaries. So I brought out fire from within you; it consumed you, and I turned you to ashes on the earth in the sight of all who saw you. All who know you among the peoples are appalled at you; you have come to a dreadful end and shall be no more forever. (Ezekiel 28: 12b-19, NRSV)[44]

The concept of fallen angels also finds direct expression in at least two books of the Old Testament Pseudepigrapha, i.e., I and II Enoch. As these books of the Old Testament Pseudepigrapha are likely to be unfamiliar to most readers, background information as to author, date of composition, and provenance is presented for each book, with the relevant passage from each book being quoted immediately after the presentation of background information.

There are three different books of the Old Testament Pseudepigrapha that are known as Enoch, i.e., I Enoch or the Ethiopian Apocalypse of Enoch, II Enoch or the Slavonic Apocalypse of Enoch, and III Enoch or the Hebrew Apocalypse of Enoch, and it is important not to confuse them. I Enoch appears to be a composite manuscript that is the result of numerous different authors who were writing across different time periods, ranging from the early second century BCE to the first century BCE. It was probably originally written in a combination of Hebrew and Aramaic by anonymous Jews of the Essenic or Pharisaic persuasion who were living in southern Palestine. While the only complete copies currently existing are in Ethiopic, fragments of I Enoch have been discovered in Aramaic, Greek,

---

[44] In this passage, the King of Tyre, perhaps Ithbaal II, is compared to a fallen cherub, i.e., Satan, who was expelled from the Garden of Eden. Brownlee WH (1971).

and Latin. While originally written as Jewish literature, I Enoch was known by many of the Church Fathers, including: (1) Saint Justin Martyr (circa 100-165 CE); (2) St. Irenaeus (circa 120-203 CE), the bishop of Lyon (177-circa 203 CE); (3) Origen (circa 185-254 CE); and (4) St. Clement of Alexandria (Titus Flavius Clemens, circa 150-215 CE). Further, I Enoch was held in high regard by Tertullian (Quintus Eptimus Florens Tertullianus, circa 155-post 220 CE). Finally, it should be noted that I Enoch influenced such books of the New Testament Apocrypha as the Epistle of Barnabas and the Apocalypse of Peter, and it was quoted by at least one New Testament author in Jude 1:14-15.[45] I Enoch also appears to have had some influence on such New Testament books as Matthew, Luke, John, Acts, Romans, I and II Corinthians, Ephesians, Colossians, I and II Thessalonians, I Timothy, Hebrews, I John, and Revelation.[46]

Drawing heavily on the previously quoted material from Genesis 6: 1-4, the authors of I Enoch developed an entire theology of fallen angels. In this theology, the fallen angels came down to earth, took and impregnated human wives, fathered giants, and taught humans forbidden science and knowledge that ended up corrupting people, e.g., how to make armaments, cosmetics, and precious metals. Although Enoch attempted to intercede on behalf of these fallen angels, his intercession was to no avail, and he ended up prophesizing the final doom of the fallen angels.[47]

> In those days, when the children of man had multiplied, it happened that there were born unto them handsome and beautiful

---

[45] Jude 1:14-15 reads as follows. "It was also about these that Enoch, in the seventh generation from Adam, prophesied, saying, 'See, the Lord is coming with ten thousands of his holy ones, to execute judgment on all, and to convict everyone of all the deeds of ungodliness that they have committed in such an ungodly way, and of all the harsh things that ungodly sinners have spoken against him.'" (NRSV)
[46] Isaac E (2011).
[47] Isaac E (2011).

daughters. And the angels, the children of heaven, saw them and desired them; and they said to one another, "Come, let us choose wives for ourselves from among the daughters of man and beget us children." And Semyaz, being their leader, said unto them, "I fear that perhaps you will not consent that this deed should be done, and I alone will become (responsible) for this great sin." But they all responded to him, "Let us all swear an oath and bind everyone among us by a curse not to abandon this suggestion but to do the deed." Then they all swore together and bound one another by (the curse). And they were altogether two hundred...

And they took wives unto themselves, and everyone (respectively) chose one woman for himself, and they began to go unto them. And they taught them magical medicine, incantations, the cutting of roots, and taught them (about) plants. And the women became pregnant and gave birth to great giants...

And Azaz'el taught the people (the art of) making swords and knives, and shields, and breastplates; and he showed to their chosen ones bracelets, decorations, (shadowing of the eye) with antimony, ornamentation, the beautifying of the eyelids, all kinds of precious stones, and all coloring tinctures and alchemy. And there were many wicked ones and they committed adultery and erred, and all their conduct became corrupt...And secondly the Lord said to Raphael, "Bind Azaz'el hand and foot (and) throw him into the darkness!" And he made a hole in the desert which was in Duda'el and cast him there; he threw on top of him rugged and sharp rocks. And he covered his face in order that he may not see light; and in order that he may be sent into the fire on the great day of judgment...

The First Sin–Religious Texts

And I, Enoch, began to bless the Lord of the mighty ones and the King of the universe. At that moment the Watchers were calling me. And they said to me, "Enoch, scribe of righteousness, go and make known to the Watchers of heaven who have abandoned the high heaven, the holy eternal place, and have defiled themselves with women, as their deeds move the children of the world, and have taken unto themselves wives: They have defiled themselves with great defilement upon the earth; neither will there be peace unto them nor the forgiveness of sin…"

As for Enoch, he proceeded and said to Azaz'el, "There will not be peace unto you; a grave judgment has come upon you. They will put you in bonds, and you will not have (an opportunity for) rest and supplication, because you have taught injustice and because you have shown to the people deeds of shame, injustice, and sin." (I Enoch 6:1-6a; 7:1-2; 8:1-2; 10:4-6; 12:3-5; 13:1-2)[48]

It should be noted that in the above passage, one of the fallen angels was named Azaz'el, which is the same name as Azazel (Leviticus 16:8-10) and as Azazil, which Ibn 'Abbas in the Islamic tradition reportedly once maintained was the original name of Satan. This may be one example of Jewish stories and traditions making their way into Islamic tradition by way of some of the companions of Prophet Muhammad relying on Jewish sources or by way of spurious fabrications creeping into some of the *Ahadith* literature. (Note: if the above passage from I Enoch 6:1-13:2 had been quoted in full, the reader would have been informed of the names of far more fallen angels than just Semyaz and Azaz'el.)

II Enoch, also known as Slavonic Enoch, presents a host of special problems when it comes to historical background. The oldest known manuscript of II Enoch is a Slavonic manuscript from the 14th century

---

[48] Isaac E (2011).

CE. As such, background information and provenance are basically reduced to scholarly inference as to the date and language of the original composition and as to the author. The range of scholarly speculation on these issues is enormous, with opinions ranging from: (1) a book written by a Hellenized Jew in Egypt in the first century BCE, to (2) a book written by a Christian monk in Byzantium in the ninth century CE. However, the most likely hypothesis is that II Enoch was originally written in either Greek or a Semitic language by a Jew writing in the late first century CE.[49]

> But one from the order of archangels deviated, together with the division that was under his authority. He thought up the impossible idea, that he might place his throne higher than the clouds which are above the earth, and that he might become equal to my power. And I hurled him out from the height, together with his angels. And he was flying around in the air, ceaselessly, above the Bottomless. (II Enoch 29:4-5)[50]

Early Christian belief also maintained that Satan was a fallen angel.[51] For example, Saint Irenaeus (circa 120-203 CE), the bishop of Lyon (177-203 CE), wrote that Satan was one of the angels who were originally placed over the spirit of the air and that he later became an apostate angel and the enemy of mankind, having separated himself from the divine law.[52] Likewise, Tertullian (Quintus Eptimus Florens Tertullianus, circa 155-post 220 CE) wrote that Satan was the "angel of evil."[53] No doubt Irenaeus and

---

[49] Andersen FI (2011).
[50] Andersen FI (2011), page 148.
[51] Smith W (---).
[52] Bercot D (1998). St. Irenaeus' statement that Satan was originally one of those angels who were placed in charge of the air may be a reference to the New Testament passage found in Ephesians 2:1-2, which reads as follows: "You were dead through the trespasses and sins in which you once lived, following the course of this world, following the ruler of the power of the air, the spirit that is now at work among those who are disobedient." (NRSV)
[53] Bercot D (1998).

The First Sin–Religious Texts

Tertullian were influenced by at least some of the following New Testament verses, the last of which specifically identifies Satan as being at the head of a group of fallen angels.

> For if God did not spare the angels when they sinned, but cast them into hell and committed them to chains of deepest darkness to be kept until the judgment… (II Peter 2:4, NRSV)

> And the angels who did not keep their own position, but left their proper dwelling, he has kept in eternal chains in deepest darkness for the judgment of the great Day. (Jude 1:6, NRSV)

> And war broke out in heaven; Michael and his angels fought against the dragon. The dragon and his angels fought back, but they were defeated, and there was no longer any place for them in heaven. The great dragon was thrown down, that ancient serpent, who is called the Devil and Satan, the deceiver of the whole world—he was thrown down to the earth, and his angels were thrown down with him. (Revelation 12:7-9, NRSV)

In contrast with the Jewish and Christian view that Satan was a fallen angel, the *Qur'an* maintains that Satan was a jinn. This is explicitly stated in *Qur'an* 18:50: "…except for Iblis, who was one of the jinns…" That Iblis was a jinn and not an angel is also implied in *Qur'an* 7:12 and 38:74 where Iblis states, "…You made me from fire…" These two verses become definitive when one compares them with the following two Qur'anic verses.

> And so it was that We created human beings from pliable clay—from mere molded mud, and We created the jinns, even before (human beings), from the intense heat (of pure energy). (*Qur'an* 15:26-27, Emerick translation)

He created human beings from molded clay, and He created jinns from smokeless fire. (*Qur'an* 55:14-15, Emerick translation)

Adam was created from mud or clay, but Iblis was part of the prior creation of jinn, a creation that was made from fire. In contrast to the jinn being created from fire and to Adam being created from mud or clay, a *Hadith* tracing back to Prophet Muhammad states that angels were created from light.

'Aisha reported that God's Messenger said: "The angels were born out of light and the jinns were born out of the spark of fire and Adam was born as he has been defined (in the *Qur'an*) for you (i.e., he was fashioned out of clay)." (*Muslim, Hadith* #7134)

This differentiation between angels and jinn is consistent with the Islamic position that angels were not granted the gift and heavy responsibility of having free will, a gift that was bestowed on both mankind and the jinn. As such, angels cannot engage in voluntary action, thus negating the possibility of sinning. Since Islam maintains that angels cannot sin, there can be no fallen angels within Islamic theology. This concept that angels do not have free will finds some support in the following Qur'anic verse describing the angels who are appointed guardians over Hell.

All you who believe! Save yourselves and your families from a fire whose fuel is men and the stone (of idols), over which are appointed stern and severe angels who don't hesitate from thoroughly carrying out the commands they receive from God, and they do whatever they're commanded. (*Qur'an* 66:6, Emerick translation)

So what exactly is a jinn? A jinn may be conceptualized as an other-dimensional being or as an elemental spirit that has certain capacities and abilities that humans do not have. For example, Islamic tradition maintains that the jinn are free of certain physical constraints and have the ability to change shape and form. However, unlike the angels, the jinn are mortal and do have basic physical needs and desires, just as humans do.

It should be noted that the Arabic word "jinn" can at times also be applied to humans, as noted by Yahiya Emerick.

> *Jinns* (genies) are elemental spirits who often seek to create mischief for physical beings. The term *jinn*, itself, which comes from the root *junna*, literally means to be *hidden* or *concealed*. Thus, the term can be applied to unseen creatures, unknown strangers or to anything that we don't see. The Arabs also referred to babies in the womb as *hidden*, or *jenin*, given that they were not seen…[54]

Arrogance and Racism

The *Qur'an* specifically attributes Satan's initial sin to arrogance. "He refused in his arrogant pride… I'm better than he is… he became proud and lost his faith… Are you too proud, or are you so high and mighty?" As was the case with the longer Qur'anic accounts of the first sin, the Jewish rendition of this event found in the Life of Adam and Eve also focuses on Satan's arrogance as a prime mover in his commission of the first sin. "I will not worship one inferior and subsequent to me. I am prior to him in creation; before he was made, I was already made. He ought to worship me." However, this arrogance as expressed in the previously quoted verses from the Life of Adam and Eve does not have the expressed racist element that is found in several of the Qur'anic passages.

> "I'm better than he is," (Iblis) replied, "for You made me from fire, while You made him from clay." (*Qur'an* 7:12, Emerick translation)

---

[54] Emerick Y (2000), page 50.

"I'm not going to prostrate myself to a mortal man," Iblis answered, "for You created him from mineral-rich clay, from mere molded mud!" (*Qur'an* 15:33, Emerick translation)

"How can I bow down to a creature that You made from mud?" he asked. (*Qur'an* 17:61, Emerick translation)

"I'm better than him,"(Iblis) answered. "You made me from fire, while You made him from clay." (*Qur'an* 38:76, Emerick translation)

In the above Qur'anic accounts, Satan reveals himself to be the first racist. Based solely on physical etiology, Satan defines himself as being of a superior category of creation than that of Adam.[55] In the Jewish version as found in the Life of Adam and Eve, it is not that Satan sees himself as being made of a superior substance than Adam, and thus being constitutionally and by nature superior to Adam. Rather, Satan's arrogance is simply in that he was made before Adam. However, in the Midrashic version of this story, the first part of which was quoted in footnote #12, the text goes on to identify the racist element in Satan's arrogance when Satan contrasts his own substance of creation (variously identified in the Midrash as the divine glory and God's Own Presence) with that of Adam (the dirt of the earth).

SATAN VS. GOD

Another difference between the Islamic and Jewish accounts is that in the Jewish version of the first sin, Satan's arrogance is not just in how he compares himself to Adam. Satan's arrogance also surfaces in his futile threat to erect his throne above the stars of Heaven and to make himself

---

[55] Emerick Y (2000), page 570, footnote 2013, in his commentary on *Qur'an* 38:76.

the equal of God. "…I will set my throne above the stars of heaven and will be like the Most High." Not only does Satan arrogantly declare himself to be Adam's superior, he also boasts in his self-conceit and ignorance that he is God's very equal!

In contrast to the unbridled arrogance the Life of Adam and Eve attributes to Satan in his threatening to be like God Himself, in the Qur'anic accounts, despite his arrogance, Satan always knows his limitations when it comes to challenging God. That this is so can be seen in the Qur'anic passages quoted below. Four different times the Qur'anic accounts have Satan asking God to give him respite until the Day of Judgment.

> "Give me time!" (Iblis) cried out. "(Give me time) until the day when they're all resurrected." (*Qur'an* 7:14, Emerick translation)

> "My Lord!" Iblis cried out. "Give me some time until they're resurrected." (*Qur'an* 15:36, Emerick translation)

> (Iblis said,) "…If you give me a chance until the Day of Assembly, I'll make his descendants blindly obedient (to me), all but a few!" (*Qur'an* 17:62, Emerick translation)

> "My Lord!" (Iblis) cried. "Give me time until the day You resurrect (them)." (*Qur'an* 38:79)

When one makes a request of another, one is acknowledging, however reluctantly, that the other is in a superior position to the one making the request. That Satan requests God to give him respite from punishment until the Day of Judgment demonstrates that Satan does, at least grudgingly, recognize that God is in a position far superior to his own. However, Satan's arrogance is still such that he apparently cannot bring himself to ask God for forgiveness and to then bow down to Adam.

The Image of God

It should be noted that the Life of Adam and Eve maintains that the angels were called upon to worship Adam because Adam was supposedly made in the very image of God. That Adam was made in the image of God is also maintained in the first creation story told in the Biblical book of Genesis, as well as in later passages in Genesis, thus having relevance for both Judaism and Christianity.

> Then God said, "Let us make humankind in our image, according to our likeness; and let them have dominion over the fish of the sea, and over the birds of the air, and over the cattle, and over all the wild animals of the earth, and over every creeping thing that creeps upon the earth." So God created humankind in his image, in the image of God he created them; male and female he created them. (Genesis 1:26-27, NRSV)

> This is the list of the descendants of Adam. When God created humankind, he made them in the likeness of God. Male and female he created them, and he blessed them and named them "Humankind" when they were created. (Genesis 5:1-2, NRSV)

> Whoever sheds the blood of a human, by a human shall that person's blood be shed; for in his own image God made humankind. (Genesis 9:6, NRSV)

It is not just in the Old Testament that Judaism and Christianity have references to mankind being created in the image of God. That concept also finds expression in two different books of the Old Testament Apocrypha, Ecclesiasticus[56] and II Esdras.[57] The relevant passages from

---

[56] Ecclesiasticus, a.k.a. the Wisdom of Jesus bin Sirach, was written in Hebrew around the year 180 BCE by Jesus bin Sirach, a Jew living in Jerusalem early in the second century BCE. Beavin EL (1971).

[57] Chapters three through 14 of II Esdras, a.k.a. IV Esdras, were originally written by an unknown Jew in Hebrew in the first century CE, while chapters one, two, and 15-16 are later Christian additions. Dentan RC (1971a).

The First Sin–Religious Texts

Ecclesiasticus and II Esdras are quoted immediately below.

> The Lord created human beings out of earth, and makes them return to it again. He gave them a fixed number of days, but granted them authority over everything on the earth. He endowed them with strength like his own, and made them in his own image. (Ecclesiasticus 17:1-3, NRSV)

> But people, who have been formed by your hands and are called your own image because they are made like you, and for whose sake you have formed all things—have you also made them like the farmer's seed? Surely not, O Lord above! But spare your people and have mercy on your inheritance, for you have mercy on your own creation. (II Esdras 8:44-45, NRSV)

Further, it should be noted that in the Christian tradition Paul appears to be referencing the story of Adam being created in the image of God when he writes a rather disparaging comparison between men and women in the New Testament book of I Corinthians. The passage in question is quoted immediately below.

> For a man ought not to have his head veiled, since he is the image and reflection of God; but woman is the reflection of man. (I Corinthians 11:7, NRSV)

What is meant by being made in the image of God? According to Robert W. Crapps, Pitts Professor of Religion, Emeritus, at Furman University, the meaning is hard to determine with any precision and can mean several different things.

> Image of God. Used in the OT (Old Testament) to indicate the distinctiveness of persons in God's created order. What constitutes human uniqueness has been the subject of considerable theological

discussion ("reason," "soul," "free will," etc.), but this is not the focus of the biblical materials...The most obvious meaning is physical resemblance, but the writer clearly intends more, suggesting a more complex relationship between Creator and human creation. It is difficult to determine what the priestly writer meant specifically...Whole persons are made in God's image; the image of God is not an implanted characteristic...both Gen 1:26-27 and 9:1-7 use image of God to indicate that humans are both different from and superior to other animals...Yet the created is not equal to the Creator. Persons are in the image of God; they are not God...Thus minimally in describing persons in the image of God the priestly writer intends to affirm a superiority over other creation and an inferiority to God as Creator...The capacity to speak is probably a part of what it means to have been created in the image and likeness of God.[58]

No such attribution that Adam was created in the image of God is made in the Qur'anic accounts of the first sin or in the Qur'anic accounts of the creation of Adam and Eve. Further, Muslims reject the implied anthropomorphism embedded in the concept that the first humans were made in the image of God. They also reject the concept that God somehow has a form, shape, or physical substance such that mankind could have been created in God's image.

THE BLAME GAME

Both the Life of Adam and Eve and the Qur'anic passages relate that having committed the first sin out of arrogance, Satan was unable or unwilling to acknowledge responsibility for and accept blame for his

---

[58] Crapps RW (1997), pages 402-403.

The First Sin–Religious Texts

own action of defiance in the face of the divine command to bow down to Adam. Rather than confess his sin and ask for divine forgiveness and mercy, Satan attempted to shift the blame for his sinful action onto another. On this point, both the Jewish and Islamic texts are in agreement. However, there is a fundamental difference between the Life of Adam and Eve and two of the Qur'anic passages when it comes to whom Satan attempts to blame for his own transgression. In the Life of Adam and Eve, Satan attempts to shift the blame for his own sinful behavior to Adam, while in the *Qur'an* Satan blames God for Satan's commission of the first sin. The relevant passages highlighting this difference are quoted below.

> And the devil sighed and said, "O Adam, all my enmity and envy and sorrow concern you, since because of you I am expelled and deprived of my glory which I had in the heavens in the midst of angels, and because of you I was cast out onto the earth…It is because of you that I have been thrown out of there." (Life of Adam and Eve 12:1; 13:1)[59]

As can be seen from the above quotation, in the Life of Adam and Eve, it is as though Satan were saying, "It's not my fault that I disobeyed. I'm blameless. Adam made me do it. It's all his fault. You can't hold me responsible for something Adam caused me to do. He's the one who should be punished. It's totally unfair to punish me. Because it's all Adam's fault, I'm going to seduce Adam and his posterity into sin. I'll get back at all mankind for what Adam did to me." In contrast, Satan's accusation in two Qur'anic passages is that it is all God's fault that Satan sinned. "…it was You Who made me slip up…"

---

[59] Johnson MD (2011), page 262.

The First Sin: Jewish, Christian, and Islamic Perspectives

Then Iblis said, "And since it was You Who made me slip up, I'll lie in wait for them on Your 'straight path.'" (*Qur'an* 7:16, Emerick translation)

"My Lord!" (Iblis) said. "Since You made me slip up, I'm going to make (immorality and wickedness) seem proper and good to those on earth, and I'm going to deviate all of them (morally)…" (*Qur'an* 15:39, Emerick translation)

It was certainly bad enough to have Satan attempting to shift the blame for the first sin onto an innocent Adam, as does the report found in the Life of Adam and Eve. However, it is totally blasphemous for Satan to blame God for Satan's own actions, as is the case in the two Qur'anic passages quoted above. It's as though Satan were saying, "You (God) caused me to slip up. I'd have never sinned on my own. It's Your fault. You've persecuted and been unjust to me. As such, I'm going to take it out on that part of Your creation known as humanity."

SATAN AND THE NARCISSISTIC PERSONALITY

Contemporary studies of psychopathology have isolated a diagnostic category known as narcissistic personality disorder, which is characterized by a number of criteria, including: (1) a pervasive pattern of grandiosity; (2) a grandiose sense of self-importance; (3) a preoccupation with fantasies of unlimited success; (4) a belief that one is special; (5) a need for excessive admiration; (6) an attitude of entitlement, in which one expects special status and privileges without accepting reciprocal responsibility; (7) a lack of empathy; (8) being envious of others or believing that others are envious of oneself; and (9) an arrogant manner. The presence of five or more of the above traits is usually considered diagnostic of a narcissistic personality disorder.[60]

---

[60] (A) Durand VM, Barlow DH (2006); (B) --- (1994).

The First Sin–Religious Texts

In reviewing the description of Satan found in both the Qur'anic accounts and in the Life of Adam and Eve, several of these criteria come immediately to mind. For example, who can doubt that the second criterion has been met when one considers the gross ego inflation and feelings of grandiosity that are evidenced in Satan's refusal to obey a command from God? As the Qur'anic texts note: "He (Satan) refused in his arrogant pride…I'm (Satan) better than he (Adam) is…he (Satan) became proud and lost his faith…Are you (Satan) too proud, or are you so high and mighty?" In the Life of Adam and Eve, Satan's grandiose sense of self-importance actually rises to the level of delusions of grandeur as he seeks to equate himself with God Almighty: "If he (God) be wrathful with me, I will set my throne above the stars of heaven and will be like the Most High." Given the sum total of the above, one can only assume that Satan's ego inflation and grandiose sense of self-importance represent a pervasive personality pattern, thus satisfying the first diagnostic criterion as well as the second.

Whether or not Satan was preoccupied with fantasies of unlimited success is unclear from the Jewish and Islamic texts, although it is obvious that Satan's challenge, recorded in the Life of Adam and Eve, to set his throne above the stars of heaven and to be like God Himself suggests the possibility of such fantasies. Further suggestions that Satan harbored fantasies of unlimited, or nearly unlimited, success can be seen in the following Qur'anic verses, in which Satan boasts of his anticipated future victories in leading mankind away from God.

> …I'll lie in wait for them on Your 'straight path.' I'll attack them from their front and their back and from their right and their left, and in the end You'll see that most of them are thankless (towards You). (*Qur'an* 7:16-17, Emerick translation)

...I'm going to make (immorality and wickedness) seem proper and good to those on earth, and I'm going to deviate all of them (morally)—except, (of course), for Your sincere servants among them. (*Qur'an* 15:39-40, Emerick translation)

If You give me a chance until the Day of Assembly, I'll make his descendants blindly obedient (to me), all but a few! (*Qur'an* 17:62, Emerick translation)

I'm going to seduce them all, except for Your sincere servants, of course. (*Qur'an* 38:82-83, Emerick translation)

With regard to the fourth feature of the narcissistic personality, i.e., a belief that one is special, how else can one account for the following. (1) Satan believed that he was superior to Adam, either by the substance from which he was created (*Qur'an*) or by having been created before Adam (Life of Adam and Eve). (2) Satan believed he was above and beyond God's command to bow down to Adam. (3) Satan believed that he could defy God's command and get away with it. These same three considerations speak directly to and satisfy the sixth criteria for a narcissistic personality, i.e., feelings of entitlement, in which one expects special status and privileges without accepting reciprocal responsibility. Finally, the ninth feature of the narcissistic personality, i.e., arrogant behavior, is clearly evident in both the Qur'anic accounts of Satan's first sin and in the Life of Adam and Eve.

Although not a criteria for diagnosing the narcissistic personality, there is a characteristic defensive strategy employed by narcissists when things go wrong for them, e.g., when external reality confronts them with their own faults or failings. Typically, they initially resort to face-saving excuses

---

[61] Millon T (1981), page 168.

and rationalizations. If these defensive maneuvers prove too feeble for the narcissist to maintain his or her illusion of superiority in the face of external reality, the narcissist is then likely to turn against others, using externalization of blame as a psychic defense mechanism.[61]

> Then Iblis said, "And since it was You Who made me slip up, I'll lie in wait for them on Your 'straight path.'...." (*Qur'an* 7:16, Emerick translation)

> "My Lord!" (Iblis) said. "Since You made me slip up, I'm going to make (immorality and wickedness) seem proper and good to those on earth, and I'm going to deviate all of them (morally)—except, (of course), for Your sincere servants among them." (*Qur'an* 15:39-40, Emerick translation)

> And the devil sighed and said, "O Adam, all my enmity and envy and sorrow concern you, since because of you I am expelled and deprived of my glory which I had in the heavens in the midst of angels, and because of you I was cast out onto the earth...It is because of you that I have been thrown out of there." (Life of Adam and Eve 12:1; 13:1)[62]

As the above passages demonstrate, unable to acknowledge his own sinful behavior and his own inadequacies and deficiencies, Satan opted for the defense mechanism of externalization of blame, projecting his own deficiencies onto either Adam (Life of Adam and Eve) or God Himself (*Qur'an*) in a pathetic attempt to maintain his inordinate ego inflation. Needless to say, such an intrapsychic maneuver makes true contrition impossible, without which one cannot seek and ask for forgiveness, thus blocking oneself off from the mercy of God.

---

[62] Johnson MD (2011), page 262.

Chapter Three
On Arrogance, Haughtiness, Pride and Self-Conceit

THE JEWISH TEXTS

Introduction

JEWISH SCRIPTURE AND LITERATURE FREQUENTLY condemn the sin of arrogance, haughtiness, pride, and self-conceit. Such condemnation is unanimously spread across the pages of the Old Testament, the *Babylonian Talmud*, and the Old Testament Apocrypha. Over and over again, these Jewish sources stress that arrogance and pride lead to destruction and that they alienate the haughty and self-conceited individual from God. In what follows, sample passages are quoted from all three sources to illustrate how negatively arrogance is portrayed in early Jewish thought.

The Old Testament

The subject of arrogance is hardly dealt with in the Torah, but both the Nevi'im and the Ketuvim roundly condemn arrogance and warn of the dangers associated with haughtiness, pride, and self-conceit. Within the Nevi'im, arrogance is clearly condemned in the Deuteronomic books,[63]

---

[63] During the seventh century BCE in the Southern Kingdom of Judah, a specific theological and scholarly tradition was emerging, which can be called the Deuteronomic School. This tradition, while demonstrating great familiarity with the prior religious practices of the Northern Kingdom of Israel, which by this time was no longer extant, was clearly a creation of the Southern Kingdom of Judah. This can be illustrated by noting the marked focus of the Deuteronomic School on the centrality of the temple cult and temple sacrifice at the Solomonic Temple in Jerusalem. In fact, this centrality of the Solomonic Temple for all aspects of religious life was one of the three primary theological constructs of the Deuteronomic School. The other two were: (1) God's relationship with Israel being one of repeated divine retribution for apostasy,

(contd. on page 45)

with the sixth-century BCE books of I and II Samuel serving as cases in point. In I Samuel 2:3, Hannah, the mother of Samuel, warns against prideful speech, while in II Samuel 22:28-29, King David offers up a song of thanksgiving in which he notes that God favors the humble while bringing down the haughty.

> Hannah (the mother of Samuel) prayed and said…"Talk no more so very proudly, let not arrogance come from your mouth…" (I Samuel 2:1 & 3, NRSV)

> You deliver a humble people, but your eyes are upon the haughty to bring them down. Indeed, you are my lamp, O Lord, the Lord lightens my darkness. (II Samuel 22:28-29, NRSV)

It is worth noting that the immediately above quoted passage from II Samuel has a close parallel statement in Psalms 18:27-28, a psalm that is traditionally attributed to King David.

> For you deliver a humble people, but the haughty eyes you bring down. It is you who light my lamp; the Lord, my God, lights up my darkness. (Psalms 18:27-28, NRSV)

Still further examples of arrogance, haughtiness, pride, and self-conceit being condemned may be found in the various books of the so-called Minor Prophets that comprise the Book of the Twelve in the Nevi'im. This is illustrated by the following quotation from Malachi,

---

(contd. from page 44)
followed by Israel's repentance, followed by God's continual forgiveness; and (2) God's unconditional fulfillment of His promises of reward to Israel, regardless of Israel's sins, faults, apostasy, and idolatry. The Deuteronomic School played a central role in the creation of the Biblical books of Deuteronomy, Joshua, Judges, I Samuel, II Samuel, I Kings, and II Kings, and thus helped to create a particular interpretation and presentation of the history of ancient Israel from the 15th through the first half of the sixth century BCE. Hyatt JP (1971).

which is perfectly general, applicable to all arrogant people, and one of the most potent castigations of arrogance to be found in the entire Nevi'im. The passage states that those who are arrogant will be subjected to a punishment by fire that will leave them as mere burnt stubble in the field, without root or branch. Whether this passage refers to the End Times or to some other intervention by God into human history is unclear.

> See, the day is coming, burning like an oven, when all the arrogant and all evildoers will be stubble; the day that comes shall burn them up, says the Lord of hosts, so that it will leave them neither root nor branch. (Malachi 4:1,[64] NRSV)

As can be seen by the above quotations from the Old Testament, the Nevi'im offers several passages that severely condemn arrogance, haughtiness, pride, and self-conceit. However, condemnation of arrogance is even more frequently encountered in the Ketuvim portion of the Old Testament. For example, the book of Job maintains that the prideful are humiliated, that kings who behave arrogantly are to be bound in fetters, that God does not regard those who are conceited, and that the proud are to be abased and brought low.

> When others are humiliated, you say it is pride; for he saves the humble. (Job 22:29, NRSV)

> He does not withdraw his eyes from the righteous, but with kings on the throne he sets them forever, and they are exalted. And if they are bound in fetters and caught in the cords of affliction, then he declares to them their work and their transgressions, that they are behaving arrogantly. (Job 36:7-9, NRSV)

---

[64] Malachi 4:1 in the Protestant Old Testament is Malachi 3:19 in the *Tanakh*.

On Arrogance, Haughtiness, Pride and Self-Conceit

> The Almighty—we cannot find him; he is great in power and justice, and abundant righteousness he will not violate. Therefore mortals fear him; he does not regard any who are wise in their own conceit. (Job 37:23-24, NRSV)

> (God said to Job:) "Pour out the overflowings of your anger, and look on all who are proud, and abase them. Look on all who are proud, and bring them low; tread down the wicked where they stand." (Job 40:11-12, NRSV)

Likewise, the book of Psalms castigates the arrogant in no uncertain terms. This is clearly illustrated in the following four verses. In them, we are told that the arrogant persecute the poor and will be caught in their own schemes, that God punishes the haughty, that people are happy when they trust in God and do not follow the proud, and that King David said that he would not tolerate the haughty and arrogant.

> In arrogance the wicked persecute the poor—let them be caught in the schemes they have devised. (Psalms 10:2, NRSV)

> The Lord preserves the faithful, but abundantly repays the one who acts haughtily. (Psalms 31:23, NRSV)

> Happy are those who make the Lord their trust, who do not turn to the proud, to those who go astray after false gods. (Psalms 40:4, NRSV)

> (David said:) A haughty look and an arrogant heart I will not tolerate. (Psalms 101:5b, NRSV)

The condemnation of arrogance also finds repeated expression in the so-called Wisdom Literature of the Ketuvim. Both Proverbs and Ecclesiastes spare no measure in condemning arrogance as a fatal character flaw.

For example, Proverbs maintains that God hates haughty eyes, pride, and arrogance, that pride brings eventual disgrace and destruction, and that God tears down the house of the proud. Even more strikingly, Proverbs goes on to say that the arrogant are an actual abomination to God, that they will suffer divine punishment, and that haughty eyes are a sin. Ecclesiastes simply notes that the patient person is better than the proud person.

> There are six things that the Lord hates, seven that are an abomination to him: haughty eyes, a lying tongue, and hands that shed innocent blood, a heart that devises wicked plans, feet that hurry to run to evil, a lying witness who testifies falsely, and one who sows discord in a family. (Proverbs 6:16-19, NRSV)

> The fear of the Lord is hatred of evil. Pride and arrogance and the way of evil and perverted speech I hate. (Proverbs 8:13, NRSV)

> When pride comes, then comes disgrace; but wisdom is with the humble. (Proverbs 11:2, NRSV)

> The Lord tears down the house of the proud, but maintains the widow's boundaries. (Proverbs 15:25, NRSV)

> All those who are arrogant are an abomination to the Lord; be assured, they will not go unpunished…Pride goes before destruction, and a haughty spirit before a fall. It is better to be of a lowly spirit among the poor than to divide the spoil with the proud. (Proverbs 16:5 & 18-19, NRSV)

> Before destruction one's heart is haughty, but humility goes before honor. (Proverbs 18:12, NRSV)

On Arrogance, Haughtiness, Pride and Self-Conceit

> Haughty eyes and a proud heart—the lamp of the wicked—are sin. (Proverbs 21:4, NRSV)

> A person's pride will bring humiliation, but one who is lowly in spirit will obtain honor. (Proverbs 29:23, NRSV)

> …the patient in spirit are better than the proud in spirit. (Ecclesiastes 7:8, NRSV)

The Old Testament does not stop in just condemning arrogance. It goes further in that it actively lauds humility, the opposite of arrogance. The following verses from the Nevi'im are representative of this. In Isaiah, God says that He resides with the humble and revives their spirit and that He looks to those who are humble and contrite. In Micah, one is directed to "walk humbly with God," while Zephaniah urges the reader to seek humility, noting that it is the humble who obey the commands of God.

> For thus says the high and lofty one who inhabits eternity, whose name is Holy: I dwell in the high and holy place, and also with those who are contrite and humble in spirit, to revive the spirit of the humble, and to revive the heart of the contrite. (Isaiah 57:15, NRSV)

> Thus says the Lord…this is the one to whom I will look, to the humble and contrite in spirit, who trembles at my word. (Isaiah 66:1-2, NRSV)

> He has told you, O mortal, what is good; and what does the Lord require of you but to do justice, and to love kindness, and to walk humbly with your God? (Micah 6:8, NRSV)

> Seek the Lord, all you humble of the land, who do his commands;

seek righteousness, seek humility; perhaps you may be hidden on the day of the Lord's wrath. (Zephaniah 2:3, NRSV)

Once again, however, it is perhaps in the Ketuvim that one finds the fullest expression of the virtues and rewards of humility. II Chronicles states that God hears the prayers of and forgives the humble. Furthermore, Psalms maintains that God leads the humble along the right path and adorns them with victory. Finally, Proverbs notes that God favors the humble and rewards them with riches, honor, and life.

> ...if my people who are called by my name humble themselves, pray, seek my face, and turn from their wicked ways, then I will hear from heaven, and will forgive their sin and heal their land. (II Chronicles 7:14, NRSV)

> He (God) leads the humble in what is right, and teaches the humble his way. (Psalms 25:9, NRSV)

> For the Lord takes pleasure in his people; he adorns the humble with victory. (Psalms 149:4, NRSV)

> The Lord's curse is on the house of the wicked, but he blesses the abode of the righteous. Toward the scorners he is scornful, but to the humble he shows favor. (Proverbs 3:33-34, NRSV)

> The reward for humility and fear of the Lord is riches and honor and life. (Proverbs 22:4, NRSV)

As can be seen, the Old Testament roundly condemns arrogance as a sin, while praising sincere humility. Those who are arrogant will be abased, disgraced, and brought down, for they are an abomination before God and are hated by God. In contrast, the humble will receive God's reward, are a pleasure to Him, and will receive the final victory.

On Arrogance, Haughtiness, Pride and Self-Conceit

The *Babylonian Talmud*

Consistent with the teachings of the Old Testament, the *Babylonian Talmud* typically condemns arrogance, haughtiness, and pride, although the immediately following passage from Tractate Sotah indicates some disagreement among the rabbis as to whether or not some small measure of pride is acceptable in the disciple of a sage, if not laudatory. However, the second quoted passage below, i.e., the one from Tractate Baba Batra, appears to settle the matter by stating that anyone who is prideful cannot be a true disciple of the sages.

> Said R. Hiyya bar Ashi…, "A disciple of a sage should have one eighth of an eighth [of pride]." Said R. Huna son of R. Joshua, "And it serves as his crown, like the fan of a grain." Said Raba, "He is subject to excommunication if there is [arrogance] in him, and he is subject to excommunication if there is no [arrogance] in him." Said R. Nahman bar Isaac, "[He should have] no part of it, nor even of part of part of it." Is it a small thing that it is written in connection [with arrogance], 'Everyone who is proud of heart is an abomination to the Lord' (Proverbs 16:5)?" (Tractate Sotah, Neusner translation)

> Said R. Judah said Rab, "Whoever takes pride in wearing the cloak of a disciple of the sages but is not really a disciple of the sages—they will not bring him in to the circle of the Holy One blessed be He." (Tractate Baba Batra, Neusner translation)

To some readers, the sum total of the above two passages may seem rather ambiguous when it comes to the issue of arrogance. However, other passages of the *Babylonian Talmud* make perfectly clear that arrogance is not to be tolerated. For example, the following four passages leave no room to doubt that the arrogant person will be leveled, diminished, brought down, and humbled.

...R. Eleazar said R. Hanina said, "...if the person grows arrogant, the Holy One, blessed be he, levels him... (Tractate Zebahim, Neusner translation)

R. Avira expounded, sometimes in the name of R. Assi and sometimes in the name of R. Ammi, "Whoever is arrogant in the end will be diminished..." (Tractate Sotah, Neusner translation)

And said R. Eleazar: "When The Holy One, Blessed Be He, designates greatness for someone, he designates it to his children and grandchildren to the end of the generations, as is said, '...and he seats them forever' (Job. 36: 7). But if he becomes haughty, The Holy One, Blessed Be He, brings him down, as is said, 'If they are tied with [ropes...He tells them what they have done...'] (Job 36: 8-9)." (Tractate Megillah, Neusner translation)

A Tannaite statement: In the name of Sumkhos they said, "Blessed are you...who humbles the haughty." (Tractate Ta'anit, Neusner translation)

Just how severely is the arrogant person to be brought down? Tractate Baba Batra states that an arrogant person is not acceptable even in his own household. Further, Tractate Sukkah maintains that arrogance is the chief reason among four reasons for legitimately confiscating someone's property. Additionally, Tractate 'Arakhin narrates that arrogance is one of seven possible causes of plagues descending upon a person.

Said R. Mari, "Someone who is arrogant is not acceptable even in his own household: 'A haughty man abides not' (Habakkuk 2:5)— A haughty man abides not—even in his own household." (Tractate Baba Batra, Neusner translation)

For four reasons is the property of householders confiscated for

On Arrogance, Haughtiness, Pride and Self-Conceit

> taxes: because of those who hold back the wages of a hired hand, because of those who oppress a hired hand, because of those who remove the yoke from their shoulders and put it on their fellow, and because of arrogance. But arrogance outweighs all the others. And with reference to humble people, it is written, "But the humble shall inherit the earth and delight themselves in the abundance of peace (Psalms 37:11)." (Tractate Sukkah, Neusner translation)

> On account of seven causes plagues come (upon someone): slander, bloodshed, a vain oath, incest, arrogance, theft, and envy. (Tractate 'Arakhin, Neusner translation)

The above passages describe the punishments that befall the arrogant person in this worldly life. However, the *Babylonian Talmud* also talks about the punishment that will befall those who are arrogant and conceited upon the Day of Resurrection. For example Tractate Sotah, while maintaining that an arrogant person is to be cut down as though he were a tree that is being worshiped as an idol, states that such a person will not even be resurrected from the grave.

> Arrogance is a vice; humility is a virtue. Whoever is arrogant in the end will be diminished. God is with the contrite and humble. Whoever is arrogant is worthy of being cut down like an *asherah* (a tree that is worshiped). Whoever is arrogant—his dust will not be stirred up in the resurrection of the dead…Concerning whoever is arrogant said the Holy One, blessed be he, he and I cannot live in the same world. Whoever is arrogant—even the slightest breeze shakes him. (Tractate Sotah, Neusner translation)

> And R. Eleazar said, "Whoever is arrogant—his dust will not be stirred up (in the resurrection of the dead). For it is said, 'Awake

and sing, you that dwell in the dust' (Isaiah 26:19). It is stated not 'You who lie in the dust,' but 'You who dwell in the dust,' meaning, one who has become a neighbor to the dust [by constant humility] even in his lifetime." And R. Eleazar said, "For whoever is arrogant the Presence of God laments, as it is said, 'But the haughty he knows from afar' (Psalms 138: 6)." (Tractate Sotah, Neusner translation)

Just how thoroughly does the *Babylonian Talmud* condemn arrogance? The answer may be found in the following passages, the first of which equates arrogance with idolatry, while the second states that the Messiah will not come until there are no longer any arrogant people in Israel. Even more dramatically, the third and fourth passages quoted immediately below state that Hell, i.e., Gehenna, will be the final abode of the arrogant, an ending far more terrifying than the previously mentioned fate of simply not being resurrected from the grave.

And R. Yohanan said in the name of R. Simeon b. Yohai, "Whoever is arrogant is as if he worships idolatry." (Tractate Sotah, Neusner translation)

...said R. Hanina, "The son of David will come only when arrogant people will no longer be (found) in Israel, as it is said, 'For then I will take away out of the midst of you those who rejoice in your pride' (Zephaniah 8:11), followed by: 'I will also leave in the midst of you an afflicted and poor people, and they shall take refuge in the name of the Lord' (Zephaniah 3:12)." (Tractate Sanhedrin, Neusner translation)

Whoever is arrogant falls into Gehenna. (Tractate Baba Batra, Neusner translation)

On Arrogance, Haughtiness, Pride and Self-Conceit

Said R. Oshaia, "Whoever takes pride falls into Gehenna: 'A proud and haughty man, scoffer is his name, works for arrogant wrath' (Proverbs 21:24), and 'wrath' means only Gehenna: 'That day is a day of wrath' (Zephaniah 1:15)." (Tractate Abodah Zarah, Neusner translations)

The arrogant person will be brought down in this life. He is not welcome in his own household, and his very arrogance is deserving of plagues and the confiscation of his property. The arrogant person is to be equated with an idolater, and he either will not be resurrected on Judgment Day or will be punished with God's wrath in Hell. Surely, this is more than enough to establish that arrogance, self-conceit, and haughtiness are to be avoided at all costs. No wonder that the rabbi prayed to be saved from the sin of arrogance.

When Rabbi had finished saying his Prayer, this is what he said: "May it be pleasing before you, O Lord our God and God of our fathers, that you save us from those who are arrogant and from arrogance, from a bad man and a bad encounter, from the evil impulse and a bad associate, from a bad neighbor and from the destructive Satan, from a bad judgment and from a difficult litigant, whether a member of the covenant or not." (Tractate Berakhot, Neusner translation)

As was the case in the Old Testament, the *Babylonian Talmud* goes beyond condemning the sin of arrogance. It also lauds humility, the opposite of arrogance. The following two passages illustrate this point.

Who is someone who will inherit the world to come? It is one who is meek and humble, who bends when he comes and bends when he goes out, who always is studying the Torah, but does not take pride in himself on that account. (Tractate Sanhedrin, Neusner translation)

There are those who say, "And he who does not raise himself with pride, others will raise him..." (Tractate Mo'ed Qatan, Neusner translation)

THE OLD TESTAMENT APOCRYPHA

It is not just in the Old Testament and the *Babylonian Talmud* that the Jewish tradition condemns pride and arrogance. The Old Testament Apocrypha repeatedly warns against pride, arrogance, haughtiness, and self-conceit. For example, Tobit states that ruin is the end result of pride, and I Maccabees[65] associates arrogance with a time of ruin and anger.

For in pride there is ruin and great confusion. (Tobit 4:13b, NRSV)

Now the days drew near for Mattathias to die, and he said to his sons: "Arrogance and scorn have now become strong; it is a time of ruin and furious anger..." (I Maccabees 2:49, NRSV)

However, it is in the so-called Wisdom Literature that one finds the most complete and thorough condemnation of arrogance, pride, haughtiness, and self-conceit that is to be found in the Old Testament Apocrypha. For example, the Wisdom of Solomon[66] rhetorically asks, "What has our arrogance profited us?" and then goes on to ask if one's boasted wealth actually brings any good. By implication, both rhetorical questions are to be answered in the negative.

---

[65] I Maccabees was originally written in Hebrew at some point between 104 and 63 BCE by a Palestinian Jew who was quite possibly a member of the Sadducee party of Judaism. Knight GAF (1971); Oesterley WOE (1971); Flusser D (2003).

[66] The Wisdom of Solomon, a.k.a. Wisdom and Book of Wisdom, was originally written in Greek, probably in Alexandria, Egypt, circa 50 BCE, with estimated dates ranging from 220 BCE to 50 CE. Dentan RC (1971b); Peacock HF (1997b).

On Arrogance, Haughtiness, Pride and Self-Conceit

> What has our arrogance profited us? And what good has our boasted wealth brought us? (Wisdom of Solomon 5:8, NRSV)

If the Wisdom of Solomon raises rhetorical questions about arrogance, Ecclesiasticus, another example of Wisdom Literature within the Old Testament Apocrypha, positively and unequivocally condemns arrogance. According to Ecclesiasticus, pride and arrogance lead many astray, are hateful to God and to other humans, lead to calamities and destruction, and prevent healing from calamities. Moreover, the very beginnings of pride are said to be the forsaking of God. These and additional condemnations of arrogance and pride are clearly stated in the following verses from Ecclesiasticus.

> For their conceit has led many astray, and wrong opinion has impaired their judgment…When calamity befalls the proud, there is no healing, for an evil plant has taken root in him. (Ecclesiasticus 3:24 & 28, NRSV)

> Arrogance is hateful to the Lord and to mortals, and injustice is outrageous to both. Sovereignty passes from nation to nation on account of injustice and insolence and wealth. How can dust and ashes be proud? Even in life the human body decays. A long illness baffles the physician; the king of today will die tomorrow. For when one is dead he inherits maggots and vermin and worms. The beginning of human pride is to forsake the Lord; the heart has withdrawn from its Maker. For the beginning of pride is sin, and the one who clings to it pours out abominations. Therefore the Lord brings upon them unheard-of calamities, and destroys them completely… Pride was not created for human beings, or violent anger for those born of women. (Ecclesiasticus 10:7-13, 18, NRSV)

Like a decoy partridge in a cage, so is the mind of the proud, and like spies they observe your weakness; for they lie in wait, turning good into evil, and to worthy actions they attach blame. (Ecclesiasticus 11:30-31, NRSV)

Whoever touches pitch gets dirty, and whoever associates with a proud person becomes like him. (Ecclesiasticus 13:1, NRSV)

She (i.e., wisdom) is far from arrogance... (Ecclesiasticus 15:8, NRSV)

Panic and insolence will waste away riches; thus the house of the proud will be laid waste. (Ecclesiasticus 21:4, NRSV)

If you open your mouth against your friend, do not worry, for reconciliation is possible. But as for reviling, arrogance, disclosure of secrets, or a treacherous blow—in these cases any friend will take to flight. (Ecclesiasticus 22:22, NRSV)

O Lord, Father and God of my life, do not give me haughty eyes... Sinners are overtaken through their lips; by them the reviler and the arrogant are tripped up. (Ecclesiasticus 23:4 & 8, NRSV)

The strife of the proud leads to bloodshed, and their abuse is grievous to hear... Mockery and abuse issue from the proud, but vengeance lies in wait for them like a lion. (Ecclesiasticus 27:15 & 28, NRSV)

Amuse yourself there to your heart's content, but do not sin through proud speech. (Ecclesiasticus 32:12, NRSV)

Just as the author of Ecclesiasticus condemns all forms of pride and arrogance, he also lauds the opposite of them. Over and over again, Ecclesiasticus informs the reader of the spiritual value and rewards of true humility. God delights in and is glorified by a person's humility, and He reveals his secrets to those who are truly humble. It is humility that results in one being loved by those close to God, and it is humility that honors oneself. Furthermore, the prayers of the humble are said to pierce the heavens, reach God, and receive God's response.

> For the fear of the Lord is wisdom and discipline, fidelity and humility are his delight. (Ecclesiasticus 1:27, NRSV)

> Those who fear the Lord prepare their hearts, and humble themselves before him. (Ecclesiasticus 2:17, NRSV)

> My child, perform your tasks with humility; then you will be loved by those whom God accepts. The greater you are, the more you must humble yourself; so you will find favor in the sight of the Lord. Many are lofty and renowned, but to the humble he reveals his secrets. For great is the might of the Lord; but by the humble he is glorified. (Ecclesiasticus 3:17-20, NRSV)

> Humble yourself to the utmost, for the punishment of the ungodly is fire and worms. (Ecclesiasticus 7:17, NRSV)

> My child, honor yourself with humility. (Ecclesiasticus 10:28, NRSV)

> The prayer of the humble pierces the clouds, and it will not rest until it reaches its goal; it will not desist until the Most High responds. (Ecclesiasticus 35:21, NRSV)

THE CHRISTIAN TEXTS

As noted in the first chapter, there is no explicitly Christian text that recounts the story of the first sin and of Satan's fall due to arrogance. Instead, one often finds the early Church Fathers attributing Satan's downfall to his envy that man was made in the very image of God while Satan was not. Thus, St. Irenaeus (circa 120-203 CE, the bishop of Lyon 177-circa 203 CE), states that Satan was envious of God's workmanship in creating Adam, decided to turn mankind into something at enmity with God, and thus became an apostate or fallen angel. Tertullian (Quintus Eptimus Florens Tertullianus, circa 155-post 220 CE) also noted that Satan deceived Adam because he envied him. Cyprian (Thascius Caecilius Cyprianus, circa 200-258, bishop of Carthage circa 248-258) also attributed Satan's fall to his envy and jealousy over man having been made in the image of God. Finally, Lactantius (Lucius Caecilius Firmianus Lactantius, circa 240-320 CE) maintained that Satan fell due to his envying that the pre-existent Jesus Christ was made of divine origin while he was not and that envy thus became the original source of all later evils.[67]

The above sources not withstanding, Christianity incorporates the Jewish texts found within the Old Testament and the Old Testament Apocrypha that were previously quoted, that roundly attack the sin of arrogance, and that praise the virtue of humility. Furthermore, the New Testament offers numerous passages that portray arrogance in a decidedly negative light. The following passages from the gospels are examples that stand in need of no commentary or elaboration.

> All who exalt themselves will be humbled, and all who humble themselves will be exalted. (Matthew 23:12, NRSV)

> For all who exalt themselves will be humbled, and those who humble themselves will be exalted. (Luke 14:11, NRSV)

> I tell you, this man went down to his home justified rather than the other; for all who exalt themselves will be humbled, but all who humble themselves will be exalted. (Luke 18:14, NRSV)

---

[67] Bercot D (1998).

On Arrogance, Haughtiness, Pride and Self-Conceit

It is not just in the gospels that the New Testament condemns haughtiness, arrogance, and self-conceit. Numerous condemnations of these traits can be found in the Pauline epistles,[68] as the following quotations illustrate.

> They were filled with every kind of wickedness, evil, covetousness, malice. Full of envy, murder, strife, deceit, craftiness, they are gossips, slanderers, God-haters, insolent, haughty, boastful, inventors of evil, rebellious toward parents, foolish, faithless, heartless, ruthless. (Romans 1:29-31, NRSV)

> ...So do not become proud, but stand in awe. (Romans 11:20, NRSV)

> Live in harmony with one another; do not be haughty, but associate with the lowly; do not claim to be wiser than you are. (Romans 12:16, NRSV)

> It is actually reported that there is sexual immorality among you, and of a kind that is not found even among pagans; for a man is living with his father's wife. And you are arrogant! Should you not rather have mourned, so that he who has done this would have been removed from among you? (I Corinthians 5:1-2, NRSV)

---

[68] "At one time, it was widely held that Paul wrote 14 letters that were incorporated into the New Testament, as well as some letters that were lost. However, at present, almost all Biblical scholars reject Pauline authorship of Hebrews, and most also reject the concept that Paul wrote I and II Timothy and Titus, while admitting that these latter three books represent Pauline thinking. In addition, many Biblical scholars see Ephesians, Colossians, and II Thessalonians as being authored by someone other than Paul, although again admitting that they reflect the Pauline approach to Christianity. The only undisputed Pauline works among modern Biblical scholars are Romans, I Corinthians, II Corinthians, Galatians, Philippians, I Thessalonians, and Philemon.

Given the above, only seven books of the New Testament can be said to be primary source material on Paul, i.e., Romans, I Corinthians, II Corinthians, Galatians, Philippians, I Thessalonians, and Philemon." Dirks JF (2011), pages 54-55.

> Love is patient; love is kind; love is not envious or boastful or arrogant… (I Corinthians 13:4, NRSV)
>
> Let us not become conceited… (Galatians 5:26, NRSV)
>
> Do nothing from selfish ambition or conceit, but in humility regard others as better than yourselves. (Philippians 2:3, NRSV)

Both the New Testament gospels and the epistles that all Biblical scholars agree were written by Paul roundly condemn arrogance. Further condemnation of arrogance is found in the remaining epistles of the New Testament. For example, James states that "God opposes the proud" and that arrogance is evil. I Timothy maintains that those who are "puffed up with conceit" may "fall into the condemnation of the devil." II Timothy demands that the arrogant are to be avoided, and I Peter states that "God opposes the proud."

> God opposes the proud, but gives grace to the humble…Humble yourselves before the Lord, and he will exalt you. (James 4:6 & 10, NRSV)
>
> Come now, you who say, "Today or tomorrow we will go to such and such a town and spend a year there, doing business and making money." Yet you do not even know what tomorrow will bring. What is your life? For you are a mist that appears for a little while and then vanishes. Instead you ought to say, "If the Lord wishes, we will live and do this or that." As it is, you boast in your arrogance; all such boasting is evil. (James 4:13-16, NRSV)[69]

---

[69] The *Qur'an* offers identical advice when it comes to qualifying one's intentions: "Never say of anything, 'I'll do it tomorrow,' without adding, 'If God wills.' If you forget (to add this phrase), then remember your Lord (when you recall your lapse) and say, 'I hope that my Lord guides me closer to the rightly guided way.'" (*Qur'an* 18:23-24, Emerick translation)

On Arrogance, Haughtiness, Pride and Self-Conceit

The saying is sure: whoever aspires to the office of bishop desires a noble task…He must not be a recent convert, or he may be puffed up with conceit and fall into the condemnation of the devil. (I Timothy 3:1 & 6, NRSV)

As for those who in the present age are rich, command them not to be haughty, or to set their hopes on the uncertainty of riches, but rather on God who richly provides us with everything for our enjoyment. (I Timothy 6:17, NRSV)

You must understand this, that in the last days distressing times will come. For people will be lovers of themselves, lovers of money, boasters, arrogant, abusive, disobedient to their parents, ungrateful, unholy, inhuman, implacable, slanderers, profligates, brutes, haters of good, treacherous, reckless, swollen with conceit, lovers of pleasure rather than lovers of God, holding to the outward form of godliness but denying its power. Avoid them! (II Timothy 3:1-5, NRSV)

For a bishop, as God's steward, must be blameless; he must not be arrogant or quick-tempered or addicted to wine or violent or greedy for gain… (Titus 1:7, NRSV)

And all of you must clothe yourselves with humility in your dealings with one another, for "God opposes the proud, but gives grace to the humble." Humble yourselves therefore under the mighty hand of God, so that he may exalt you in due time. (I Peter 5:5-6, NRSV)

Several of the above quoted verses not only disparage arrogance, but they also laud humility and meekness. The holding up of humility as a character trait that is to be cultivated is also found in numerous other verses of the New Testament. For example, the gospels twice have Jesus directly commending meekness and humility.

> Blessed are the meek, for they will inherit the earth. (Matthew 5:5, NRSV)

> Whoever becomes humble like this child is the greatest in the kingdom of heaven. (Matthew 18:4, NRSV)

The lauding of humility is also emphasized in the following passages from the New Testament epistles. Of the three passages quoted below, the first two passages are from epistles that may or may not have been authored by Paul, although they were certainly written in the Pauline tradition.

> I therefore, the prisoner in the Lord, beg you to lead a life worthy of the calling to which you have been called, with all humility and gentleness, with patience, bearing with one another in love... (Ephesians 4:1-2, NRSV)

> As God's chosen ones, holy and beloved, clothe yourselves with compassion, kindness, humility, meekness, and patience. (Colossians 3:12, NRSV)

> Finally, all of you, have unity of spirit, sympathy, love for one another, a tender heart, and a humble mind. (I Peter 3:8, NRSV)

THE ISLAMIC TEXTS

THE *QUR'AN*

Like the Jewish and Christian literature, the *Qur'an* is quite explicit in warning people not to be arrogant. In that regard, people are reminded of their limitations and frailties. Further, they are told that arrogance leads to eventual ruin, a ruin from which there is no escape if proper repentance has not been made prior to the final death rattle. Unfortunately, arrogance

On Arrogance, Haughtiness, Pride and Self-Conceit

too often prevents a person from repenting—"he denied and turned away and then strutted arrogantly back to his family."

> Don't strut through the earth acting like you're so great, for (you're not strong enough) to rip the earth apart, nor can you grow as tall as mountains. (*Qur'an* 17:37, Emerick translation)

> …when (a dying soul) reaches the collarbone at last…(It'll be too late for repentance then), for he never donated, nor did he pray. Rather, he denied and turned away and then strutted arrogantly back to his family. You're ruined—ruined! Once more, you're mruined—ruined! (*Qur'an* 75:26, 31-35, Emerick translation)

Pride and arrogance interfere with a person's ability to believe in and worship God. In contrast to that state of affairs, the *Qur'an* informs people that true believers are never too arrogant to worship God. True believers recognize God's majesty and power, preventing them from falling into haughty self-conceit. They live a life of humility, both in their relationship with God and with their fellow man.

> The true believers are those who, when they hear Our verses being read out to them, fall down in adoration and praise of their Lord. They're never too proud (to bow down before their Lord). (*Qur'an* 32:15, Emerick translation)

> The (true) servants of the Compassionate are those who walk humbly through the earth. Whenever the ignorant try to engage them (in futile argument), they say to them, "Peace." (*Qur'an* 25:63, Emerick translation)

> Isn't it time for the hearts of the believers to humble themselves to the remembrance of God? (*Qur'an* 57:16, Emerick translation)

In contrast to the true believers, unbelievers are often full of arrogance, for arrogance interferes with a person's ability to have appropriate belief in God and to recognize and believe in His signs. As noted in the following verse, the arrogant person who lacks proper belief in God forfeits his inborn ability to see and recognize God's signs. As such, he inevitably goes astray.

> And I shall steer away from My signs those who act arrogantly in the earth against all right. Even if they see the signs, they're not going to believe in them, and even if they see the path of common sense, they're not going to adopt the way. Rather, if they see any way to go astray, that's the path they'll choose. (*Qur'an* 7:146, Emerick translation)

Qur'an 85:14 states that God is "the Forgiving and Loving," and *Qur'an* 11:90 notes that God is full of "loving tenderness." While these attributes of God cannot be doubted, the *Qur'an* also states that the arrogant and conceited person forfeits God's love for him.

> God has no love for conceited snobs… don't despair over what you've lost or brag about what you've gained, for God has no love for conceited show offs. (*Qur'an* 4:36, 57:23, Emerick translation)

> Don't puff up your cheek (arrogantly) at other people nor strut around through the earth, for God has no love for conceited snobs. (*Qur'an* 31:18, Emerick translation)

> Your God is One God. Those who have no faith in the next life have stubborn hearts, and they're arrogant besides! Without a doubt God knows what they're (doing both) in secret and out in the open, and He has no love for the arrogant… (*Qur'an* 16: 22-23, Emerick translation)

On Arrogance, Haughtiness, Pride and Self-Conceit

Having forfeited God's love for him, the arrogant person also cuts himself off from God's guidance, mercy, and forgiveness. He is left adrift without the benefit of divine guidance, and he then loses the ability to differentiate right from wrong. Even when he can discern right from wrong, his arrogance leads him further astray.

> "Don't cry out (for mercy) today!" (they'll be told,) "for you'll find no help from Us! My (revealed) verses were read out to you, but you used to turn back on your heels arrogantly, saying bad things about them like a storyteller in the night." (*Qur'an* 23:65-67, Emerick translation)

> When they're told, "Come, let the Messenger of God pray for your forgiveness," you see them turning their heads aside and slipping away arrogantly. It's all the same whether you pray for their forgiveness or not; God won't forgive them, for God doesn't guide the rebellious. (*Qur'an* 63:5-6, Emerick translation)

Having been warned against being arrogant and having been informed that ruin is the final lot of the arrogant, those who persist in arrogant and haughty pride and self-conceit forfeit God's love for them. Thus, they also cut themselves off from God's guidance, mercy, and forgiveness. Left alone to their own devices, arrogant people walk down a sinful path that eventually leads to God's punishment. That punishment is their eventual fate is repeatedly stressed in the *Qur'an*.

> Whoever arrogantly refuses to serve Him will be gathered back to Him (for judgment)… those who were hesitant and arrogant will be punished by Him with a painful punishment, and they'll find no one to help them or protect them besides God! (*Qur'an* 4:172-173, Emerick translation)

If you could only see how the corrupt will be during the confusion of their death throes. The angels will reach out with their hands (and say), "Away with your souls. This day you'll get your payment—a humiliating punishment on account of your saying things about God against all right and because you arrogantly (rejected) His signs!" (*Qur'an* 6:93, Emerick translation)

There are some among people who buy useless tales that are devoid of knowledge, in order to mislead others from the path of God by making a mockery of (knowledge). They'll have a humiliating punishment. When Our (revealed) verses are read out to such a one, he turns away arrogantly, acting like he didn't hear anything—almost like he was deaf in both ears! Give him the news of a terrible punishment! (*Qur'an* 31:6-7, Emerick translation)

On that day they'll indeed share in the punishment all together, for that's how We deal with the wicked. They became arrogant whenever they were told that there's no god but the (One True) God…" (*Qur'an* 37:33-35, Emerick translation)

Ruin to every sinful charlatan! He hears the signs of God enumerated for him; yet, he becomes stubborn and arrogant, acting as if he never heard them! Tell him about a painful punishment! (*Qur'an* 45:7-8, Emerick translation)

The faithless boast, "We're never going to believe in this Qur'an nor in any other (scriptures) that came before it." If you could only see it—when the wrongdoers will be made to stand before their Lord. They'll be blaming each other back and forth! The lowly (masses will be yelling) at their arrogant (leaders), saying, "If it weren't for you, then we would've been believers!"

On Arrogance, Haughtiness, Pride and Self-Conceit

> Those arrogant (leaders) will answer the lowly (masses) saying, "Were we the ones who held you back from (God's) guidance after it came to you? No way! You were (perfectly willing) to be wicked yourselves!" The lowly (masses) will reply, "Not so! It was your (plan all along when you told us every) day and night to reject God and to make others equal with Him!"
>
> When they see the punishment (that awaits them), they're going to be speechless in their remorse. Then We'll drape (iron) collars around the necks of those who suppressed (their faith), for they deserve no less for their deeds. (*Qur'an* 34:31-33)

Being cut off from God's love, guidance, mercy, and forgiveness is certainly, in and of itself, a painful punishment, although a person's arrogance may blind him to that fact. However, the punishment for arrogance is not confined to what is lost or forfeited. The ultimate punishment for arrogance will be assigned on Judgment Day, and that punishment is eternal confinement in Hell. Just as the *Qur'an* repeatedly warns that arrogance will be punished, it also repeatedly stresses that the ultimate penalty for arrogance is Hell.

> When he's told, "Be mindful of God," his arrogance causes him to go on sinning even harder. Hellfire is punishment enough for him—what a terrible place to rest! (*Qur'an* 2:206, Emerick translation)

> Those who suppress (their ability to recognize the truth of) Our (revealed) verses and (even worse) treat them in a haughty manner will be companions of the Fire, and that's where they're going to stay…Those who suppress (their ability to recognize the truth of) Our (revealed) verses and (even worse) treat them in a haughty

manner will find no opening in the gates of the sky, nor will they ever enter Paradise—no, not until a twisted rope can pass through the eye of a needle! That's Our way of paying back the wicked! Their resting place will be under layers and layers of Hellfire, and that's how We pay back wrongdoers! (*Qur'an* 7:36, 40-41, Emerick translation)

The companions of the Heights will recognize familiar men (down in Hellfire) by their features and will ask them, "What has all your hoarding and arrogance done for you now?" (*Qur'an* 7:48, Emerick translation)

(God tells the disbelievers on Judgment Day:) "But no! My signs came to you, and you denied them. You were arrogant, and you tried to cover (the truth that was all around you.)" On the Day of Assembly, you're going to see those who told lies against God with darkened faces. Isn't Hellfire the residence of the arrogant?...Then (the sinners) will be told, "Enter the gates of Hell and remain there. Oh, how terrible is the home of the arrogant!" (*Qur'an* 39:59-60, 72, Emerick translation)

The Hour (of Judgment) will definitely arrive, and there's no doubting it. Yet, even still most people don't believe (in it), even though your Lord says, "Call upon Me! I will answer you! Those who are too proud to serve Me will find themselves in humiliating Hellfire!" (*Qur'an* 40:59-60, Emerick translation)

One might think that the above passages from the *Qur'an* would be enough of a warning to mankind that arrogance leads to the damnation of Hell. However, as the following verses illustrate, the *Qur'an* relentlessly repeats again and again this dire warning.

On Arrogance, Haughtiness, Pride and Self-Conceit

(They'll be told), "This (is your fate) because in the world you looked approvingly upon everything else (but the truth), and you were brazen (in your arrogance)! So enter the gates of Hellfire, and stay inside. Oh, how terrible is the home of the arrogant!" (*Qur'an* 40:75-76, Emerick translation)

The faithless, however, (will be told), "Weren't Our signs ever presented to you? Oh, but you were arrogant and inclined towards evil. When you were told that God's promise was true and that there was no mistaking the reality of the Hour, you said, 'We don't know anything about this 'Hour.' It's nothing but a fancy notion, and we have no confidence in its (reality.)'"

Then they're going to see the (amount of) wickedness that they've amassed, and they'll be surrounded by what they used to ridicule! They'll be told, "Today We're going to forget you, just like you forgot the appointment on this day of yours! Your home is in the Fire, and no one will ever help you. You used to take the (revealed) verses of God as a joke, and the physical life of the world deceived you." From that day onward they'll never be released from it, nor will they ever have their repentance accepted. (*Qur'an* 45:31-35, Emerick translation)

On the day when the faithless will be placed by the Fire, (they're going to be told), "You had your good things in the life of the world, and you had a good time with them, but today you're going to be paid back (for your failures) with a humiliating punishment, for you were arrogant in the world - for no good reason - and you behaved poorly." (*Qur'an* 46:20, Emerick translation)

(Then the command will come), "Throw every arrogant one who suppressed (their faith in God) into Hellfire, all those who prevented good and acted aggressively, who instilled doubt and made others equal with God. Throw him into the most severe punishment (imaginable)!" (*Qur'an* 50:24-26, Emerick translation)

On the Day of Assembly they can bear their own burdens in full, as well as the burden (of the crime they committed against) the unsuspecting (people) whom they misled! Oh, how terrible the burdens they will bear!...

(Then the doomed sinners) will offer their abject submission, saying, "We didn't do anything wrong (intentionally)." (However, it will be said to them), "That's not true, for God knows what you were doing. So enter into the gates of Hellfire, and stay in there!" The home of the arrogant is an awful one indeed! (*Qur'an* 16: 25, 28-29, Emerick translation)

Before concluding the Qur'anic account regarding Hell being the final resting place of the haughty and arrogant, one final passage should be noted. In the following passage, the person being referenced, i.e., the one who turned away arrogantly, saying that the *Qur'an* was nothing more than residual magic from the distant past, is said to have been either Abu Jahl ibn Hisham, who was a distant uncle of Prophet Muhammad, or Walid ibn Mughirah.[70]

He pondered, and he schemed (against Me), so now he's doomed! Oh, how he schemed! Once again, he's doomed! Oh, how he schemed! Then he looked around (and saw the truth of God's signs), but then he frowned and scowled, turning arrogantly away,

---

[70] Emerick Y (2000), page 722.

On Arrogance, Haughtiness, Pride and Self-Conceit

saying, "This (*Qur'an*) is no more than some remnant of the magic of ancient days. This is no more than the speech of a mortal man!"

Soon will I roast him in a burning blaze—and how can you understand what that burning blaze is? It leaves nothing unscathed nor leaves anything alone! (It reduces) mortal men (to a lifeless, blank) slate, and there are nineteen (guardian angels watching) over (Hellfire). (*Qur'an* 74:18-30, Emerick translation)

The *Ahadith*

It is not just in the *Qur'an* that Islam warns against and condemns arrogance, haughtiness, self-conceit, and pride. The sayings of Prophet Muhammad continue this theme and elaborate on it. For example, Prophet Muhammad noted that there are many things that are neutral, or even positive, in and of themselves, which become a source of sin if one becomes proud of them. The following four *Ahadith* are illustrative of this teaching.

God's Messenger said: "Horses may be used for three purposes. For one man they may be a source of reward (in the Hereafter), for another a means of protection, and for another a source of sin…For the man who keeps them just out of pride and for showing off, they are a source of sin." (*Bukhari*, Volume 9, *Hadith* #454; see also *Bukhari*, Volume 6, *Hadith* #486 and *Malik*, *Hadith* #951)

Abu Dharr narrated that God's Messenger said…"The three whom God hates are an old man who commits fornication, a poor man who is proud, and a rich man who is oppressive." (*Tirmidhi*, *Hadith* #601)

'Abdullah ibn Amr ibn Al-'As narrated that God's Messenger said: "Eat, drink, give charity, and wear (good) clothes so long as neither extravagance nor pride is mixed up with it." (*Tirmidhi, Hadith* #1161)

Abu Jurayy Jabir ibn Salim Al-Hujaymi narrated that the Messenger of God said: "Have your lower garment halfway down your shin; if you cannot do it, have it up to the ankles. Beware of trailing the lower garment (on the ground), for it is conceit, and God does not like conceit." (*Abu Dawud, Hadith* #4073)

As the last quotation illustrates, God dislikes the conceit that is involved when one arrogantly wears one's clothes so long that they drag on the ground. Further, Prophet Muhammad said that such a conceited and arrogant person will be snubbed by God on the Day of Resurrection.

'Abdullah ibn 'Umar narrated that the Messenger of God said: "Whoever drags his clothes (on the ground) out of pride and arrogance, God will not look at him on the Day of Resurrection." (*Bukhari*, Volume 7, *Hadith* #683; see also *Bukhari*, Volume 5, *Hadith* #17 & Volume 7, *Ahadith* #674-675; and *Malik, Ahadith* #1633-1636)

Abu Huraira narrated that God's Messenger said: "God will not look on the Day of Resurrection at a person who drags his lower garment (behind him) out of pride and arrogance." (*Bukhari*, Volume 7, *Hadith* #679)

In other words, since God will not even look at him, the person described immediately above will be cut off from God's mercy on the Day of Judgment. The enormity of this is realized when one understands that receiving God's mercy is an indispensable factor in achieving personal salvation. According to Islam, no person can possibly earn his way into Heaven, as one's balance of good and bad deeds will always fall short of the mark. Thus, in the final analysis, one is always dependent upon God's mercy.

> 'Abdullah ibn Mas'ud narrated that the Messenger of God said: "He who lets his garment trail during prayer out of pride, God, the Almighty, has nothing to do with pardoning him and protecting him from Hell." (*Abu Dawud, Hadith* #637)

A person's pride and arrogance in this worldly life create a barrier on the Day of Judgment between him and God's mercy and protection. As such, the ultimate fate of the arrogant person is Hell. In this regard, Prophet Muhammad once said that even a mustard seed's amount of pride can prevent a person from entering Paradise! Needless to say, this is in marked contrast to the fate of the humble person who dies free from pride. So long as the humble person is a believer who strives to do good, he will be rewarded with Paradise.

> 'Abdullah ibn Mas'ud narrated: "The Messenger of God observed, 'He who has in his heart the weight of a mustard seed of pride shall not enter Paradise.' A person (among his hearers) said, 'Verily, a person loves that his dress should be fine and his shoes should be fine.' He (the Prophet) remarked, 'Verily, God is graceful, and He loves grace. Pride is disdaining the truth (out of self-conceit) and contempt for the people.'"(*Muslim, Hadith* #164; see also *Muslim, Ahadith* #165-166 and *Abu Dawud, Hadith* #4080)

> Thawban narrated that God's Messenger said, "If anyone dies free from pride, unfaithfulness regarding spoil, and debt, he will enter Paradise." (*Tirmidhi, Hadith* #873)

Haritha ibn Wahb Al-Khuzai narrated that the Prophet said: "Shall I inform you about the people of Paradise? They comprise every obscure, unimportant, humble person...Shall I inform you about the people of the Fire? They comprise every cruel, violent, proud and conceited person." (*Bukhari*, Volume 8, *Hadith* #97; see also Bukhari, Volume 6, *Hadith* #440, & Volume 8, *Hadith* #651; see also *Muslim, Ahadith* #6833-6835)

Abu Huraira narrated that the Prophet said: "Paradise and Hellfire argued, and Hell said, 'I have been given the privilege of receiving the arrogant and the tyrants.' Paradise said, 'What is the matter with me? Why do only the weak and the humble among the people enter me?' On that, God said to Paradise, 'You are My mercy that I bestow on whomever I wish of My servants.' Then God said to Hell, 'You are My punishment by which I punish whomever I wish of my slaves, and each of you will have its fill.'" (*Bukhari*, Volume 6, *Hadith* #373; see also *Bukhari*, Volume 9, *Hadith* #541, & *Muslim, Ahadith* #6818-6822)

The above statements of Prophet Muhammad are hardly the only ones relating to the final destination of those who are arrogant, full of pride, haughty, and conceited. Several other sayings of Prophet Muhammad reiterate that Hell will be the final abode of the arrogant. Therein, they will suffer a myriad of torments, the like of which we cannot even imagine.

Abu Huraira narrated that God's Messenger said: "On the Day of Resurrection, there will issue from Hell a portion having two eyes that see, two ears that hear, and a tongue that speaks, and it will say it has been put in charge of three classes: everyone who is proud and obstreperous, everyone who invokes another god along with God, and those who make representations of things." (*Tirmidhi, Hadith* #1183)

On Arrogance, Haughtiness, Pride and Self-Conceit

The above *Hadith* lists people who are proud and obstreperous as being a separate class in Hell, but one that ranks with: those who worship someone or something other than God; and "those who make representations of things," e.g., the makers of idols. Pride and self-conceit are listed right alongside of false worship and idolatry! The warning against pride and arrogance in the above *Hadith* could not be clearer. However, there are other *Ahadith* that continue this admonition. For example, in the following two *Ahadith*, it is said that on the Day of Resurrection, the proud and arrogant will be resurrected having the small size of ants, will be stepped on and humiliated, will be driven to the hottest fire of Hell, and will also suffer other torments.

> 'Abdullah ibn Amr ibn Al-'As narrated that God's Messenger said: "The proud will be resurrected like specks on the Day of Resurrection in the form of men, covered all round with humiliation. They will be driven to a prison in Hell called Bulas, with the hottest fire rising over them, and will be given to drink the liquid of the inhabitants of Hell, which is Tinat Al-Khabal." (*Tirmidhi*, *Hadith* #1321)

> The Prophet said, "The arrogant people will be gathered on the Day of Judgment reduced to the size of ants, yet in the likeness of people. Everyone will be stepping on them, humiliating them, until they enter a prison in Hellfire called Bulas. There they'll be fed flames from a fire and given a drink made from the paste of pure insanity that drips from the people of the Fire." (*Ahmad*)[71]

---

[71] Emerick Y (2000), page 584.

THE FIRST SIN: JEWISH, CHRISTIAN, AND ISLAMIC PERSPECTIVES

SUMMARY

The *Qur'an* warns people not to become puffed up with pride, for pride and arrogance are too likely to keep a person from embracing true belief, bowing down before God, and repenting of his sins. As such: "...God has no love for conceited show offs...God has no love for conceited snobs...and He has no love for the arrogant..." Such a person has sacrificed God's mercy and forgiveness on the altar of self-conceit, and he will be judged accordingly. Hell is his final destination and abode. As Prophet Muhammad noted, a mustard seed's amount of pride and arrogance is enough to bar the door to Paradise, and Hell has "been given the privilege of receiving the arrogant..."

At this point, it should be noted that Islam does not just condemn arrogance. It also lauds humility and modesty. In fact, modesty is one of the fundamental cores of Islam. That this is so can be seen in the following statements of Prophet Muhammad.

> The Messenger of God said: "Each faith had a virtue of its own, and the virtue of Islam is modesty." (*Malik, Hadith* #1615)

> The Messenger of God...said: "...Modesty is the essence of faith." (*Malik, Hadith* #1616; see also *Abu Dawud, Hadith* #4777)

> 'Imran ibn Husain reported the Messenger of God as saying, "Modesty is good altogether," or he said, "Modesty is altogether good." (*Abu Dawud, Hadith* #4778)

> 'Iyad ibn Himar reported the Messenger of God as saying: "God has revealed to me that you must be humble, so that no one oppresses another and boasts over another." (*Abu Dawud, Hadith* #4877; see also *Riyad Us-Saliheen, Hadith* #1589)

On Arrogance, Haughtiness, Pride and Self-Conceit

In closing this section, one can profitably turn to the words of Sufyan ibn 'Uyaynah (725-810 or 815 CE). Ibn 'Uyaynah was a prominent Islamic scholar who was given the title of Shaykh Al-Islam. He specialized in Qur'anic commentary and in the sayings of Prophet Muhammad. In addressing the issue of arrogance, Sufyan ibn 'Uyaynah once wrote the following.

> If a person's sin is due to desire, then have hope for him. However, if a person's sin is due to pride, then fear for him, because Prophet Adam disobeyed God due to desire, and he was forgiven, but Iblis (Satan) sinned due to pride, and he was cursed.[72]

CONCLUSIONS

As should be clear by now, there is great uniformity in the Jewish, Christian, and Islamic texts in condemning the character traits of arrogance, haughtiness, pride, and self-conceit. All three religions stress that arrogance is to be avoided, that it is evil, that God opposes the proud and haughty, and that the arrogant person will be brought down and humbled. Further, both Jewish and Islamic texts indicate that arrogance is the pathway to Hell. Finally, it should be noted that all three religions laud humility and modesty as being character traits of the true believer.

---

[72] Emerick Y (2000), page 167.

Chapter Four
Arrogance in Race

INTRODUCTION

AS SEVERAL OF THE PASSAGES quoted from the *Qur'an* in chapter two illustrate, a primary aspect of Satan's arrogance was his maintaining that he was better than Adam because he had been created from smokeless fire while Adam had merely been created from mud. Quite simply, there is no other way to classify such a statement other than being racism. As such, this chapter stops to examine the Jewish, Christian, and Islamic teachings regarding racism and ethnic bigotry, two despicable traits that often serve as deeply flawed rationales for man's inhumanity to man.

JEWISH SCRIPTURE ON RACISM

THE OLD TESTAMENT APOCRYPHA

According to some passages of Jewish scripture, racism is not only justifiable, it is actually ordained. This can be seen in a story of Noah and his three sons, Shem, Japheth, and Ham. As the story reported in Genesis goes, Noah planted a vineyard after the flood, harvested the grapes, and made wine. The Genesis story then goes on to maintain that having imbibed to excess from the wine he had made, Noah became drunk and passed out, a situation that Islam denies that any prophet would ever enter. According to the Genesis story, in his unconscious state, Noah reportedly moved in such a way as to expose himself. Ham, the father of Canaan, saw his exposed father and went and told his two brothers. Out of respect for their father, Shem and Japheth picked up a garment, walked backwards to Noah, and covered him with the garment without looking at his nakedness. When Noah awoke and discovered that Ham had seen his nakedness,

Arrogance in Race

Noah reportedly cursed Ham's son Canaan, relegating him and his descendants to perpetual slavery to the descendants of Shem and Japheth.[73]

> When Noah awoke from his wine and knew what his youngest son had done to him, he said, "Cursed be Canaan; lowest of slaves shall he be to his brothers." He also said, "Blessed by the Lord my God be Shem; and let Canaan be his slave. May God make space for Japheth, and let him live in the tents of Shem; and let Canaan be his slave." (Genesis 9:24-27, NRSV)

Pro racist sentiments can also be found in other books of the Torah. For example, both Numbers and Deuteronomy offer passages that fuel a markedly racist sentiment. The account in Numbers 25:1-5 tells of a plague that was assaulting the Israelites because of Israelite intermarriage with Moabites[74] who led their Israelite spouses into idol worship. The story then goes on to talk about an Israelite man named Zimri who married a Midianite[75] woman named Cozbi. Because of this interethnic marriage, Phinehas murdered both Zimri and Cozbi, thus reportedly earning from God the covenant of a perpetual priesthood for himself and his descendants.

> Just then one of the Israelites came and brought a Midianite woman into his family, in the sight of Moses and in the sight of

---

[73] As Ham reportedly was the eponymous ancestor of the Hamitic people, i.e., the people of sub-Saharan Africa, one interpretation of the story recounted in Genesis 9:20-27 was that Noah's curse also resulted in the skin of Ham and his descendants being turned black. Of note, Genesis 9:20-27 and the above interpretation of it were used with great frequency by the churches of the 19th-century American South in attempting to justify the slavery of Africans and of African Americans

[74] The Moabites were an ancient people who descended from Moab, their eponymous ancestor. According to Genesis 19:30-38, Moab was the son of Lot, the nephew of Abraham.

[75] The Midianites were the descendants of Midian, whom Genesis 25:1-4 identifies as being the son of Abraham and Keturah.

the whole congregation of the Israelites, while they were weeping at the entrance of the tent of meeting. When Phinehas son of Eleazar, son of Aaron the priest, saw it, he got up and left the congregation. Taking a spear in his hand, he went after the Israelite man into the tent, and pierced the two of them, the Israelite and the woman, through the belly. So the plague was stopped among the people of Israel. Nevertheless those that died by the plague were twenty-four thousand. The Lord spoke to Moses, saying: "Phinehas son of Eleazar, son of Aaron the priest, has turned back my wrath from the Israelites by manifesting such zeal among them on my behalf that in my jealousy I did not consume the Israelites. Therefore say, 'I hereby grant him my covenant of peace. It shall be for him and for his descendants after him a covenant of perpetual priesthood, because he was zealous for his God, and made atonement for the Israelites.'" (Numbers 25:6-13, NRSV)

While some might want to argue that the above passage from Numbers only has relevance for mixed marriages in which the non-Israelite leads the Israelite into idolatry, the following passage from Deuteronomy makes clear the racism and ethnic bigotry that were directed against those Israelites who entered into a mixed marriage. As this passage clearly notes, no Ammonite[76] or Moabite can be admitted to the assembly of the Lord. This was also to be the case for any descendants of an Ammonite or Moabite, even if married to an Israelite, for up to 10 generations of descent! Still further, while the Israelites were not to "abhor" the Edomites [77] and

---

[76] According to Genesis 19:36-38, the Ammonites were the descendants of Ben-ammi, the son of Lot, the nephew of Abraham.
[77] According to Genesis 36:1-14, the Edomites were the descendants of Esau (aka Edom) the older twin brother of Jacob, the son of Isaac, the son of Abraham.

Arrogance in Race

Egyptians, their descendants from a marital union with an Israelite were to be excluded from the religious assembly until the third generation. If the Edomites were the kin and friends of the Israelites, and if the Egyptians were the friends of the Israelites, then with friends like that, who needs enemies?

> No Ammonite or Moabite shall be admitted to the assembly of the Lord. Even to the tenth generation, none of their descendants shall be admitted to the assembly of the Lord…You shall never promote their welfare or their prosperity as long as you live. You shall not abhor any of the Edomites, for they are your kin. You shall not abhor any of the Egyptians, because you were an alien residing in their land. The children of the third generation that are born to them may be admitted to the assembly of the Lord. (Deuteronomy 23:3, 6-8, NRSV)

The above passage from Deuteronomy is not simply a racist aberration in an otherwise non-racist Old Testament. In that regard, consider the case of Nehemiah, the fifth-century BCE Israelite governor of the Persian province of Judaea in southern Palestine. Having traveled from the Israelite colony in exile in Babylonia, he was appalled at the state of interethnic marriage that was so commonplace among the Israelites remaining in Judaea. Among his religious reforms were edicts regarding ethnic purity and the prohibition of mixed marriages. A single passage from the fourth-century BCE book of Nehemiah serves to illustrate these reforms and edicts.

> In those days also I saw Jews who had married women of Ashdod, Ammon, and Moab; and half of their children spoke the language of Ashdod, and they could not speak the language of Judah, but spoke the language of various peoples. And I contended with them and cursed them and beat some of them and pulled out their

hair; and I made them take an oath in the name of God, saying, "You shall not give your daughters to their sons, or take their daughters for your sons or for yourselves..." (Nehemiah 13:23-25, NRSV)

As racist as the reforms of Nehemiah were, the racism and bigotry were only to increase upon the arrival of Ezra in Judaea circa 397 BCE. Of note, Ezra brought with him from Babylonia a copy of the recently completed Torah. Ezra quickly set about quoting and misquoting the Torah to further his goals of ethnic purity. Going a step beyond Nehemiah, Ezra demanded that all Israelites immediately separate themselves from any non-Israelite spouse and from any children of mixed ethnic descent.

> Now on the twenty-fourth day of this month the people of Israel were assembled with fasting and in sackcloth, and with earth on their heads. Then those of Israelite descent separated themselves from all foreigners, and stood and confessed their sins and the iniquities of their ancestors... On that day they read from the book of Moses in the hearing of the people; and in it was found written that no Ammonite or Moabite should ever enter the assembly of God...When the people heard the law, they separated from Israel all those of foreign descent (Nehemiah 9:1-2, 13:1, 3, NRSV)

The above passage is obviously alluding to Deuteronomy 23:3-8. However, Ezra manages to misquote the passage in question. In so doing, he extends the Deuteronomic School prohibition against those of Moabite or Ammonite descent from entering the religious assembly until after the 10th generation of descent to a prohibition in perpetuity.

One final passage deserves to be quoted verbatim about Ezra's role in the early fourth-century BCE edicts concerning the propagation, via a total prohibition against marrying a non-Israelite, of the myth of Israelite racial and ethnic purity. The following passage is highly significant in that it makes explicit the Israelite myth that their inheritance from Abraham, i.e., their inheritance of the land of Palestine, is based upon their alleged ethnic purity. The relevant part of the passage regarding inheritance of the land of Palestine and Israelite ethnic purity has been placed in *italics*.

> At the evening sacrifice I got up from my fasting, with my garments and my mantle torn, and fell on my knees, spread out my hands to the Lord my God, and said, "O my God, I am too ashamed and embarrassed to lift my face to you, my God, for our iniquities have risen higher than our heads, and our guilt has mounted up to the heavens…For we have forsaken your commandments, which you commanded by your servants the prophets, saying, 'The land that you are entering to possess is a land unclean with the pollutions of the peoples of the lands, with their abominations. They have filled it from end to end with their uncleanness. Therefore *do not give your daughters to their sons, neither take their daughters for your sons, and never seek their peace or prosperity, so that you may be strong and eat the good of the land and leave it for an inheritance to your children forever.*'…" While Ezra prayed and made confession, weeping and throwing himself down before the house of God, a very great assembly of men, women, and children gathered to him out of Israel; the people also wept bitterly. Shecaniah son of Jehiel, of the descendants of Elam, addressed Ezra, saying, "We have broken faith with our God and have married foreign women from the peoples of the land, but even now there is hope for Israel in spite of this. So now let us make a covenant with our God to send away all these wives and their children, according to the counsel of my lord and of those who tremble at the commandment of our God; and let it be done

according to the law. Take action, for it is your duty, and we are with you; be strong, and do it." Then Ezra stood up and made the leading priests, the Levites, and all Israel swear that they would do as had been said. So they swore. (Ezra 9:5-6, 10b-12; 10:1-5, NRSV)

It was in response to the above situation that Ezra called the Men of the Great Assembly, a group responsible for the formulation and compilation of much of the *Tanakh*. However, their primary role was not scriptural, and it did not involve the collection and collating of scripture. Instead, their primary role was in safeguarding ethnic purity. In fact, their primary job was the prohibition of future, and the dissolution of past, cases of interethnic marriage. In that regard, the Men of the Great Assembly spent three whole months, i.e., from the first day of the 10th month until the first day of the first month, compiling a list of every Israelite then living who was of mixed ethnic descent!

> Ezra the priest selected men, heads of families, according to their families, each of them designated by name. On the first day of the tenth month they sat down to examine the matter. By the first day of the first month they had come to the end of all the men who had married foreign women…All these had married foreign women, and they sent them away with their children. (Ezra 10:16b-17, 44, NRSV)

It must be emphasized that, despite later attempts to "theologize" a cover story, the marital prohibition was against marrying someone from a different ethnic group, and it was not a prohibition against marrying a non-believer. The truncated list in Ezra 10:16-44, as compiled by Ezra and the Men of the Great Assembly, said absolutely nothing about issues of religious affiliation. Its only concern was the issue of ethnic descent.

Against the racist backdrop painted by the above passages from the Old Testament, one shining story stands out in sharp counterpoint. This is the story of Ruth, a Moabite woman who had married an Israelite who was living in Moab with his brother and his parents, Elimelech and Naomi. While living in Moab, Naomi's husband and her two sons died, leaving her without any means of support. Her Moabite daughter-in-law Ruth demonstrated rare care and generosity to Naomi, leaving her own Moabite people behind and accompanying Naomi back to Israel where Ruth worked in the fields of Boaz, harvesting grain to support her mother-in-law. When Boaz saw Ruth and her dutiful nature to Naomi, he married Ruth. The union produced a son Obed, who later fathered Jesse, the father of King David. Ironically, given the prohibition in Deuteronomy 23:3-8, this meant that King David, his son King Solomon, and several generations of the kings of the Southern Kingdom of Judah should have been excluded from the "assembly of the Lord."

THE OLD TESTAMENT APOCRYPHA

Despite the anti-racist sentiments expressed in Ruth, the overall tenor of the Old Testament is racist, and that racist tinge is carried over into the Old Testament Apocrypha. For example, II Esdras 8:69-96 presents an elongated version of Ezra 9:5-10:5. In this lengthy passage from II Esdras, intermarriage is categorized as a sin and iniquity that was prohibited by God Himself, and it is said to be the reason that God allowed the Israelites to be conquered by a foreign power. As a result, in a totally heartless and racist act, the Israelites of Ezra's time decided to send away and abandon their non-Israelite spouses and the children they had by those spouses.

However, it is not just in II Esdras that the Old Testament Apocrypha supports a racist ideology. In the fourth chapter of Tobit, an Israelite father advises his son that he must never marry a non-Israelite woman.

Beware, my son, of every kind of fornication. First of all, marry a woman from among the descendants of your ancestors; do not marry a foreign woman, who is not of your father's tribe; for we are the descendants of the prophets. Remember, my son, that Noah, Abraham, Isaac, and Jacob, our ancestors of old, all took wives from among their kindred. They were blessed in their children, and their posterity will inherit the land. So now, my son, love your kindred, and in your heart do not disdain your kindred, the sons and daughters of your people, by refusing to take a wife for yourself from among them. (Tobit 4:12-13a, NRSV)

PSEUDEPIGRAPHA

The Old Testament Pseudepigrapha continues the racist theme found in both the Old Testament and the Old Testament Apocrypha. For example, in Jubilees, it is said that while Abraham's sons would be the fathers of many nations, only his descendants through Jacob, the son of Isaac, would become a "holy seed," "the portion of the Most High," and the Lord's special possession.

> And through Isaac a name and seed would be named for him. And all of the seed of his [Abraham's] sons would become nations. And they would be counted with the nations. But from the sons of Isaac one would become a holy seed and he [Jacob] would not be counted among the nations because he would become the portion of the Most High and all his seed would fall (by lot) into that which God will rule so that he might become a people (belonging) to the Lord, a (special) possession from all people, and so that he might become a kingdom of priests and a holy people. (Jubilees 16:17-18)[78]

---
[78] Wintermute OS (2011), page 88.

SUMMARY

While the story of Ruth represents a strong non-racist departure from the rest of the Old Testament, from the Old Testament Apocrypha, and from the Old Testament Pseudepigrapha, the overall theme of the Jewish scripture and ancient literature is one that is decidedly racist in its orientation.

CHRISTIANITY ON RACISM

The New Testament gospels allege that Jesus occasionally modified Old Testament teachings.[79] That is certainly the case with his reported teachings regarding non-Israelites. In that regard, consider Jesus' parable of the Good Samaritan. In that story, an Israelite was beaten, robbed, and left by the side of the road to die. Tragically, an Israelite priest and an Israelite of the tribe of Levi passed by the battered and helpless Israelite without so much as providing the least amount of help for their fellow Israelite. Finally, a man of the Samaritans, a group of mixed Israelite and foreign heritage that was generally despised by the Israelites and that practiced what the Israelites considered to be a heretical brand of Judaism, stopped and cared for the man, took him to an inn, and before leaving paid the innkeeper to nurse the Israelite back to health. Concluding the parable and driving home the need to get beyond racist and ethnic stereotypes, Jesus reportedly asked which of the three travelers was a true neighbor to the stricken Israelite.

> Jesus replied, "A man was going down from Jerusalem to Jericho, and fell into the hands of robbers, who stripped him, beat him, and went away, leaving him half dead. Now by chance a priest was going down that road; and when he saw him, he passed by on

---

[79] For example, see Matthew 5:28-41 and Luke 6:29 for how Jesus reportedly modified the Lex Talionis, i.e., the law of retaliation in kind.

the other side. So likewise a Levite, when he came to the place and saw him, passed by on the other side. But a Samaritan while traveling came near him; and when he saw him, he was moved with pity. He went to him and bandaged his wounds, having poured oil and wine on them. Then he put him on his own animal, brought him to an inn, and took care of him. The next day he took out two denarii, gave them to the innkeeper, and said, 'Take care of him; and when I come back, I will repay you whatever more you spend.' Which of these three, do you think, was a neighbor to the man who fell into the hands of the robbers?"

He (the lawyer) said, "The one who showed him mercy."

Jesus said to him, "Go and do likewise." (Luke 10:30-37, NRSV)

A second teaching against racial and ethnic pride is attributed by the New Testament to John the Baptist and revolves around his admonishment of the Pharisees and Sadducees of his day. In the following passage, John the Baptist condemns their reliance for salvation on their ethnic descent from Abraham and instructs them that they will be judged not on their racial and ethnic lineage, but on their deeds and works.

But when he saw many Pharisees and Sadducees coming for baptism, he said to them, "You brood of vipers! Who warned you to flee from the wrath to come? Bear fruit worthy of repentance. Do not presume to say to yourselves, 'We have Abraham as our ancestor'; for I tell you, God is able from these stones to raise up children to Abraham. Even now the ax is lying at the root of the trees; every tree therefore that does not bear good fruit is cut down and thrown into the fire." (Matthew 3:7-10, NRSV; see also Luke 3:7-9)

Arrogance in Race

The author of the Epistle to the Colossians, whether that was Paul or an early adherent to the Pauline school of thought, also struck a decidedly anti-racist stance. The author of the following passage argued that racial, ethnic, and nationalistic differences should be erased and eradicated and that all believers in Christ are one in Christ.

> In that renewal there is no longer Greek and Jew, circumcised and uncircumcised, barbarian, Scythian, slave and free; but Christ is all and in all! (Colossians 3:11, NRSV)

ISLAM ON RACISM

Given that the Qur'anic accounts of the first sin clearly link Satan's arrogance to racism, it should not be surprising that Islamic literature, both the *Qur'an* and the sayings of Prophet Muhammad, affirms the oneness of all of mankind and condemns the sort of ethnic and racial considerations that lead to bigotry and prejudice. It is not race or ethnicity that is the measure of a person; the worth of a person is defined by his piety and devotion to God. The following passages from the *Qur'an* serve as cases in point.

> All you people! We created you from a single (pair of) a male and a female and made you into different races and tribes so you can come to know one another. The noblest among you in the sight of God is the one who is the most mindful (of his duty to Him). (*Qur'an* 49:13, Emerick translation)

> All people were once a single community, and God raised messengers among them to give glad tidings (of Paradise) and also warnings (of Hellfire). He also sent the scriptures of truth to be a judge between people in their disputes. However, after the clear evidence came to them, those who received these (earlier) revealed

messages, out of factionalism and pride, fell into disagreement. Yet, by His grace, God guided sincere believers out of their disputes and brought them to the truth, for God guides whomever He wants towards a straight path. (*Qur'an* 2:213, Emerick translation)

And what were people other than one community (in the beginning)... (*Qur'an* 10:19, Emerick translation)

The above Qur'anic passages amply illustrate Islam's condemnation of racism and ethnic bigotry. Moreover, like the above quoted passage from Colossians 3:11, the Qur'an emphasizes that all true believers are brothers and sisters to each other. They comprise one family in faith, a family that eradicates all racial and ethnic barriers.

Truly, this community of yours is one community, and I am your Lord, so serve me. (*Qur'an* 21:92, Emerick translation)

(All you who believe!) Truly, this community of yours is one community, and I am your Lord, so be mindful of Me. (*Qur'an* 23:52, Emerick translation)

Truly, all believers are a single brotherhood, so patch things up between your brothers, and be mindful of God so you can receive mercy. (*Qur'an* 49:10, Emerick translation)

However, it is not just in the *Qur'an* that Islam condemns racism while affirming the essential unity of all mankind, especially of all believers. Similar sentiments can be found in the teachings of Prophet Muhammad. The following *Hadith* serves to illustrate this fact.

Abu Huraira reported the Messenger of God as saying: "God, Most High, has removed from you the pride of the pre-Islamic period and its boasting in ancestors. One is only a pious believer or a miserable sinner. You are sons of Adam, and Adam came from dust. Let the people cease to boast about their ancestors. They are merely fuel in Hell, or they will certainly be of less account with God than the beetle that rolls dung with its nose." (*Abu Dawud, Hadith* #5097)

While the above statement is a clear and direct refutation of racism and ethnic prejudice, an even more stringent rebuke of racism and ethnic bigotry is to be found in Prophet Muhammad's Farewell Sermon. In this address, the relevant portion of which is quoted below, the Prophet stressed that all mankind comprises a single family in descent from Adam, that ethnicity and skin color say nothing about the worth of a person, and that a person's worth is defined by his consciousness of God.

> All you people, indeed your Lord is One and your ancestor is one. All of you belong to the line of Adam, and Adam was created from dust. An Arab is not better than a non-Arab, nor is a white better than a black, nor a black better than a white except in consciousness (of God). The best among you is the one who is the most conscious of God.[80]

RACISM VS. ANTI-RACISM: A SUMMARY STATEMENT

As has been shown, Jewish scripture and the Old Testament Apocrypha portray a decidedly racist mindset that is only occasionally punctuated with anti-racist sentiments. In contrast, the Christian New Testament and the Islamic literature, both the *Qur'an* and the sayings of Prophet Muhammad, strike a decidedly anti-racist posture. More specifically, the *Qur'an* stresses that all of humanity comprises one family in descent from Adam and that all believers are brothers and sisters of each other.

---

[80] Emerick Y (2000), page 636.

Chapter Five
Arrogance in Religion

INTRODUCTION

WHILE THE *QUR'AN* DOES NOT mention Satan's arrogance in terms other than his racism, Islamic traditions tracing back to the companions[81] of Prophet Muhammad frequently indicate that Satan's arrogance also derived from the self-pride that he took in his own religious knowledge and practice.[82] According to these traditions, Satan was a great scholar and priest among the jinn, and he had been elevated to a status akin to the angels by dint of his enormous worship of God.[83] Due to the fervor of his religious practice and to the depth of his religious knowledge, Satan was allowed to live with the angels,[84] to be one of the keepers of Paradise,[85] and to be ruler over all between Heaven and Earth.[86] Further, in his capacity as ruler of all that was between Heaven and Earth, Satan was the judge and arbiter over all the other jinn.[87]

The jinn were the first creation to have free will and to live on Earth. Islamic traditions tracing to the companions of Prophet Muhammad maintain that the jinn eventually abused their free will and began to engage in corruption, bloodshed, and murder. As such, it was said that God sent

---

[81] The list of companions of Prophet Muhammad who narrated one or more elements of these traditions includes 'Abdullah ibn 'Abbas (d. 687) and 'Abdullah ibn Masud (d. 653), among others.
[82] (A) Ibn Kathir I (2000), volume 1, page 194, commentary on *Qur'an* 2:34; (B) Al-Tabari M (1989), pages 254 and 256.
[83] (A) Ibn Kathir I (2000), volume 1, page 194, commentary on *Qur'an* 2:34; (B) Usmani SA (1992), volume 1, pages 17 and 652, commentary on *Qur'an* 2:34 and 7:11-18, and volume 2, page 1356, commentary on *Qur'an* 18:50; (C) Al-Tabari M (1989), page 257.
[84] Usmani SA (1992), volume 3, page 1996, commentary on *Qur'an* 38:74-85.
[85] Al-Tabari M (1989), pages 249-250, 252-253, 256.
[86] Al-Tabari M (1989), pages 249-251, 253, 256.
[87] Al-Tabari M (1989), pages 256-257.

ARROGANCE IN RELIGION

Satan with an army of angels to wage war against the jinn. During this war, Satan and his army reportedly killed many sinful jinn and banished the rest of them to islands in the oceans and to mountainsides. Having thus fulfilled his religious duty to God in a most zealous way, Satan became even more arrogant with regard to his religious practice and knowledge.[88]

THE ISLAMIC PERSPECTIVE

In the above scenario, Satan's arrogance was based, at least in part, in his excessive religious practice, in his religious extremism, and in his holier-than-thou attitude. With regard to excessive religious practice and religious extremism, the *Qur'an* chastises those Jews and Christians who have exceeded the boundaries of proper religious belief and practice and entered the realm of religious excess.

> Followers of Earlier Revelation! Don't go to extremes in your religious (doctrines), and don't make statements about God that aren't true. (*Qur'an* 4:171, Emerick translation)

> Then say to them, "Followers of Earlier Revelation! Don't go beyond the boundaries in your way of life without any justification, nor should you follow the fickle whims of the nations who went astray before you, for they've misled many from the even way." (*Qur'an* 5:77, Emerick translation)

In the preceding verses, Jews and Christians are explicitly warned not to "go to extremes in your religious (doctrines)" and not to "go beyond the boundaries in your way of life." Likewise, both the *Qur'an* and the sayings of Prophet Muhammad urge Muslims to be moderate in their religious practice and to avoid excess in their religious practice and beliefs.

---

[88] Al-Tabari M (1989), pages 252-253.

And so it is that We have made you into a moderate community so you can be a witness to all people, even as the Messenger is a witness to you. (*Qur'an* 2:143, Emerick translation)

God's Messenger said: "...do good deeds properly, sincerely, and moderately...and always adopt a middle, moderate, regular course whereby you will reach your target (Paradise)." (*Bukhari*, volume 8, *Hadith* #470)

As can be seen from the above, Islam instructs Muslims to be moderate in their religious practice and devotion and to refrain from the sort of excessive worship and religious study that contributed to Satan's arrogance. In that regard, Prophet Muhammad refrained from excessive religious practice. Further, he taught that God actually turns away from people when they push themselves in their religious practice to the point of weariness. Excessive religious practice and devotion are seen as leading to actual ruin.

'Aisha, the wife of God's Messenger, said that whenever he had to choose between two things, he adopted the easier one, provided it was no sin. But if it was any sin, he was the one who was the farthest from it of the people... (*Muslim, Hadith* #5752; see also *Ahadith* #5753-5755)

'Aisha reported God's Messenger as saying, "Choose such actions as you are capable of performing, for God does not grow weary till you do." (*Mishkat Al-Masabih*, volume 1, page 259)

Abu Huraira narrated that the Prophet said, "This religion is very easy, and whoever overburdens himself in his religion will not be able to continue in that way. So you should not be extremists, but try to be near to perfection and receive the good tidings that you will be rewarded; and gain strength by worshiping in the mornings, afternoons, and during the last hours of the nights." (*Bukhari*, volume 1, *Hadith* #38)

Abu Huraira reported God's Messenger as saying, "The religion is ease, but if anyone overdoes, it gets the better of him..." (*Mishkat Al-Masabih*, volume 1, page 259; see also *Riyad Us-Saliheen*, *Hadith* #145)

Ibn Masud narrated that the Holy Prophet said: "Ruined are those who insisted on hardship in matters of faith." He said this three times. (*Riyad Us-Saliheen, Hadith* #144)

While the above *Ahadith* are general indictments against the arrogance of taking one's religious practice to extremes, both the *Qur'an* and the *Ahadith* literature give numerous examples of specific acts of excessive religious practice that must be avoided. In that regard, it should be noted that prayer is one of the five mandatory pillars of religious practice in Islam and that all Muslims of reasoning age are required to offer five prayers of worship each day. Nonetheless, Islam teaches that one's prayers should not be overdone.

(Muhammad!) Don't recite (the Qur'an) in your prayers too loudly or too softly, but recite in an even tone in between the two extremes. (*Qur'an* 17:110, Emerick translation)

Anas reported: The Messenger of God said: "Observe moderation in prostration (in prayer)..." (*Muslim, Hadith* #997)

Narrated 'Aisha: "Once the Prophet came while a woman was sitting with me. He said, 'Who is she?' I replied, 'She is so and so,' and told him about her (excessive) praying. He said disapprovingly, 'Do (good) deeds that are within your capacity (without being overtaxed), as God does not get tired (of giving rewards), but (surely) you will get tired, and the best deed (act of worship) in the sight of God is that which is done regularly.'" (*Bukhari*, volume 1, *Hadith* #41; see also *Bukhari*, volume 2, *Hadith* #251B and *Riyad Us-Saliheen*, *Hadith* #142)

Narrated Anas bin Malik: "Once the Prophet entered the mosque and saw a rope hanging in between its two pillars. He said, 'What is this rope?' The people said, 'This rope is for Zainab who, when she feels tired, holds it (to keep standing for the prayer).' The Prophet said, 'Don't use it. Remove the rope. You should pray as long as you feel active, and when you get tired, sit down.'" (*Bukhari*, volume 2, *Hadith* #251a; see also *Riyad Us-Saliheen*, *Hadith* #146)

Anas reported God's Messenger as saying, "One should pray as long as he is lively, but when he slackens he should stop." (*Mishkat Al-Masabih*, volume 1, page 259)

Not only did Prophet Muhammad instruct his followers to avoid excessive prayer, he also practiced moderation when it came to the length of his own prayers and to the length of his sermons. The following *Hadith* is illustrative of this fact.

On the authority of Abi 'Abdullah Jabir ibn Samura who reported: "I used to pray with the Messenger of God, and his prayer was of moderate length, and his sermon too was of moderate length." (*Riyad Us-Saliheen*, *Hadith* #148)

Another of the five pillars of religious practice in Islam is fasting from dawn to sunset during the Islamic month of Ramadan. During this time, a Muslim must refrain from the intake of all food and drink, as well as from sexual activity. However, Islam's emphasis on moderation in religious practice is exemplified in the exceptions that are made for the ill, the traveler, young children, pregnant and nursing women, etc.

> So when you see the new moon (signaling the start of Ramadan), fast the entire month, though the very ill and those traveling should fast (later when it's more convenient to do so), for God wishes ease and not hardship. (*Qur'an* 2:185, Emerick translation)

While the fast of Ramadan is mandatory on those Muslims who are physically capable of doing it, some other fasting is optional, although recommended. However, here again, Prophet Muhammad taught moderation and instructed people not to engage in continuous fasting. Further, he specifically chided those whose religious arrogance might tempt them to engage in excessive fasting.

> 'Aisha said: "The Prophet called 'Uthman bin Mas'un. When he came to him, he said: '…Fear God; 'Uthman, your wife has a right on you; your guest has a right on you; your self has a right on you. You should keep fast and (sometimes) leave fast, and pray and sleep.'" (*Abu Dawud, Hadith* #1364)

> Narrated 'Abdullah bin Amr: "God's Messenger was informed that I had said: 'By God, I will fast all the days and pray all the nights as long as I live.' On that, God's Messenger asked me. 'Are you the one who says: 'I will fast all the days and pray all the nights as long as I live?" I said, 'Yes, I have said it.' He said, 'You cannot do that. So fast (sometimes), and do not fast (sometimes). Pray and sleep. Fast for three days a month, for the reward of a good deed is multiplied by ten times, and so the fasting of three days a month equals the fasting of a year.' I said, 'O God's Messenger! I can do (fast) more than this.' He said, 'Fast on every third day.' I said: 'I

can do (fast) more than that.' He said: 'Fast on alternate days, and this was the fasting of David, which is the most moderate sort of fasting.' I said, 'O God's Messenger! I can do (fast) more than that.' He said, 'There is nothing better than that.'" (*Bukhari*, volume 4, *Hadith* 629; see also *Bukhari*, volume 3, *Ahadith* 196-197, and volume 8, *Hadith* #155)

Ibn 'Umar said that the Messenger of God forbade uninterrupted fasting… (*Muslim, Hadith* #2426; see also *Ahadith* #2427-2435, 2587-2589, & 2591-2599)

A third basic pillar of Islamic practice, i.e., *Zakat*, is the giving of a percentage of one's agricultural production and excess wealth in mandatory charity. Over and above whatever *Zakat* a Muslim owes, supplemental charity is also recommended. However, here again, both the *Qur'an* and Prophet Muhammad warned that one should not go to extremes.

Don't tie your hand to your neck (like a miser), nor extend it out so far (in donating) that you become guilty (of causing your own) poverty. (*Qur'an* 17:29, Emerick translation)

The true servants of the Compassionate…When they spend (in charity), they're neither extravagant nor stingy but maintain a position in between. (*Qur'an* 25:63a, 67, Emerick translation)

Amir bin Sad narrated that his father said, "…the Prophet paid me a visit while I was suffering from an ailment that had brought me to the verge of death. I said, 'O God's Messenger! My sickness has reduced me to the (bad) state as you see, and I am a rich man, but have no heirs except one daughter. Shall I give 2/3 of my property in charity?' He said, 'No.' I said, 'Then 1/2 of it?' He said, 'Even 1/3 is too much, for to leave your inheritors wealthy is better than to leave them in poverty, begging from people…'" (*Bukhari*, volume 8, *Hadith* 384)

While prayer, fasting, and charity represent three of the five basic pillars of Islamic religious practice, in all three cases, Prophet Muhammad taught that one should avoid extremism in going beyond reasonable limits. Further, he also instructed Muslims to avoid excessive extremes in their reading and recitation of the *Qur'an*.

'Abdullah ibn 'Amr reported: "The Messenger of God said to me: 'Recite the whole of the Qur'an during every month.' I said: 'I find power (to recite it) in a shorter period.' He said: 'Then recite it in twenty nights.' I said: 'I find power (to recite it in a shorter period even than this).' Whereupon he said: 'Then recite it in seven (nights), and do not exceed beyond it.'" (*Muslim, Hadith* #2589)

Embedded within the *Ahadith* literature are numerous other examples where Prophet Muhammad taught moderation in religious practice and the avoidance of religious extremism. The following *Ahadith* represent a few of those examples.

Narrated Anas bin Malik: "A group of three men came to the houses of the wives of the Prophet asking how the Prophet worshipped (God), and when they were informed about that, they considered their worship insufficient… Then one of them said, 'I will offer the prayer throughout the night forever.' The other said, 'I will fast throughout the year and will not break my fast.' The third said, 'I will keep away from women and will not marry forever.' God's Messenger came to them and said, 'Are you the same people who said so-and-so? By God, I am more submissive to God and more afraid of Him than you; yet, I fast and break my fast, I do sleep, and I also marry women. So he who does not follow my tradition in religion is not from me (not one of my followers).'" (*Bukhari*, volume 7, *Hadith* #1; see also *Riyad Us-Saliheen*, *Hadith* #143)

The Messenger of God said, "In this community, there will be some people who will exceed the limits in purification as well as in supplication." (*Abu Dawud*, *Hadith* #96)

On the authority of Ibn 'Abbas who said: "While the Holy Prophet was preaching, a man was standing. He (the Prophet) asked who he was. He was told that he was Abu Isra'il who had taken a vow to stand and not to sit, go into the shade, or speak, but he fasts. The Messenger of God said, 'Command him to speak, go into the shade, sit, and complete his fast.'" (*Riyad Us-Saliheen*, *Hadith* #152)

Like all great religions, Islam is built on two axes. The vertical axis represents man's relationship with God. The horizontal axis consists of man's relationship with his fellow man and with all of God's created beings. Religious arrogance and excessive religious practice and worship often lead to an overly exclusive focus on the vertical axis while ignoring or shortchanging the horizontal axis. In that regard, Prophet Muhammad taught that when an excessive focus on the vertical axis results in deficits on the horizontal axis, the rewards usually associated with worship and the fulfillment of the religious duties of the vertical axis are transferred to others.

Narrated Anas: "We were with the Prophet (on a journey), and the only shade one could have was the shade made by one's own garment. Those who fasted did not do any work, and those who did not fast served the camels and brought the water to them and treated the sick and (wounded). So the Prophet said, 'Today, those who were not fasting took (all) the reward.'" (*Bukhari*, volume 4, *Hadith* #140)

A group of the Prophet's companions approached him one day and started praising the religious devotion of a man they knew. They said of him, "We've never seen someone like him. While we travel, he recites the Qur'an at all times, and whenever we camp somewhere, we always find him engaged in prayer." The Prophet asked them, "Who took care of his baggage and fed his camel and flocks while he was at prayer?" The people replied that it was they who did these things for him. Thereupon the Prophet said, "Then you are all better than he." [89]

Finally, Islam condemns the arrogance associated with a holier-than-thou attitude. The great Sufi poet Jalaluddin Rumi, who died in 1273, wrote:

> An arrogant person will see someone do a sin, and then the fires of Hell will well up within him (in his anger about what he saw). But while he's busy calling his fiery arrogance a defense of the religion, all the while he fails to notice his own arrogant soul. (*Mathnawi* I, 3347-3348)[90]

THE CHRISTIAN PERSPECTIVE

The New Testament gives a very explicit warning against religious arrogance in words attributed to Jesus. Embedded within the so-called Sermon on the Mount, the Gospel of Matthew reports that Jesus admonished his listeners by telling them not to judge others and not to attempt

---

[89] Emerick Y (2000), page 637. The source for this *Hadith* is Ibn Qutaibeh's *Ouun Al-Akhbar*.
[90] Emerick Y (2000), page 129.

to correct the minute moral and religious errors of their contemporaries while having major faults themselves. In the reported words of Jesus, the latter form of religious arrogance is nothing short of hypocrisy.

> Do not judge, so that you may not be judged. For with the judgment you make you will be judged, and the measure you give will be the measure you get. Why do you see the speck in your neighbor's eye, but do not notice the log in your own eye? Or how can you say to your neighbor, "Let me take the speck out of your eye," while the log is in your own eye? You hypocrite, first take the log out of your own eye, and then you will see clearly to take the speck out of your neighbor's eye. (Matthew 7:1-5, NRSV; see also Luke 6:37-42)

THE JEWISH PERSPECTIVE

The *Babylonian Talmud* offers three passages that frown upon, if not condemn, religious arrogance. These three passages were quoted earlier in chapter three, but deserve to be quoted again at this juncture. The first of the three passages to be quoted below focuses on whether or not religious arrogance may be acceptable in a disciple studying religion under a renowned sage. While this passage may be somewhat ambiguous in its condemnation of religious arrogance, the second and third passages quoted below offer no equivocation in their condemnation of religious arrogance.

> Said R. Hiyya bar Ashi…, "A disciple of a sage should have one eighth of an eighth [of pride]." Said R. Huna son of R. Joshua, "And it serves as his crown, like the fan of a grain." Said Raba, "He is subject to excommunication if there is [arrogance] in him, and he is subject to excommunication if there is no [arrogance] in him." Said R. Nahman bar Isaac, "[He should have] no part of it, nor even of part of part of it." Is it a small thing that it is written

in connection [with arrogance], 'Everyone who is proud of heart is an abomination to the Lord' (Proverbs 16:5)?" (Tractate Sotah, Neusner translation)

Said R. Judah said Rab, "Whoever takes pride in wearing the cloak of a disciple of the sages but is not really a disciple of the sages—they will not bring him in to the circle of the Holy One blessed be He." (Tractate Baba Batra, Neusner translation)

Who is someone who will inherit the world to come? It is one who is meek and humble, who bends when he comes and bends when he goes out, who always is studying the Torah, but does not take pride in himself on that account. (Tractate Sanhedrin, Neusner translation)

To be always studying the Torah is a most admirable behavior for any devout Jew. However, the last quoted passage makes clear that one dare not take pride in studying the Torah. Clearly, that would be religious arrogance, and religious arrogance is to be avoided at all costs.

CONCLUSIONS

As can be seen by the sum total of the above, all three Abrahamic faiths condemn religious arrogance to a greater or lesser extent. As such, it is perplexing and extremely disheartening to note that adherents of all three faiths have at times allowed their religious arrogance and zealotry to lead them to commit untold atrocities and to engage in needless and inexcusable wars and bloodshed. Throughout the pages of history, one sees countless examples of the abominations brought on by religious arrogance. The following is only a brief and partial listing of such atrocities.

The Biblical book of Joshua recounts the genocide of the idol-worshiping and polytheistic Canaanites, Amorites, etc. as the Israelites invaded

Palestine. That such genocide was the result of religious arrogance can be seen by the fact that the Israelites believed that their mass slaughter of the inhabitants of Palestine was ordained by God against non-believers, as witnessed by the Torah's Deuteronomy 20:16-18.

A second example of the abominations that can spring from religious arrogance can be found in the Crusades. On November 25, 1095, Pope Urban II directed the Christians of Western Europe to "exterminate this vile race (of Muslims) from our lands (i.e., Palestine)." In the resulting Crusades, Jews, Muslims, and Eastern Christians were systematically slaughtered by the Western Christian Crusaders because they had different religious beliefs than did Western Christianity. For example, when Muslim Jerusalem fell to the Crusaders on July 15, 1099, between 40,000 and 70,000 Muslim, Jewish, and Eastern Christian inhabitants of Jerusalem were killed. Additionally, at Bilgays in 1168, the entire population of the city was killed by the victorious Crusaders.[91]

As a third example, consider the thousands of Jews and Muslims who were tortured or put to death by the Spanish Inquisition's attempt to force Christian conversions on its victims. Under the direction of Tomas de Torquemada, the first inquisitor general of the Spanish Inquisition, approximately 13,000 Jews were killed through the torture and execution meted out by the Inquisition. Further, many more Jews were killed later on during the Inquisition. Likewise, thousands of Muslims were sold into slavery, tortured, or killed on account of their faith.[92]

The atrocities committed through religious arrogance are not, however, limited to the distant and dusty pages of history. Whenever a holier-than-thou attitude raises its ugly head, the abuse and persecution of one religion

---

[91] Dirks JF (2004).
[92] Dirks JF (2008).

by another is likely to follow. The events of September 11, 2001, the Boston Marathon bombings, the excesses of the Taliban in Afghanistan, and the burning of *Qur'ans* and the hate-filled, anti-Islamic rhetoric by certain ministers of the extreme Christian Right all serve as stark examples that the evils associated with religious arrogance are still with us today.

What is the solution? Obviously, at least one part of the solution is to abandon religious arrogance in all its forms. Mutual tolerance and respect among adherents to different faiths must be the order of the day, and religious freedom must be observed and respected. In that regard, the following passage from the *Qur'an* offers guidance to all people, whatever their religious affiliation. In a nutshell, it instructs Prophet Muhammad to say to the unbelievers that they are entitled to their way of religious life, just as he is to his.

> Say (to them), "Hey, all you who suppress (your awareness of the truth)! I don't serve what you serve, and you don't serve what I do. And I won't serve what you serve, nor will you serve what I do—to you, your way of life, and to me, mine." (*Qur'an* 109:1-6, Emerick translation)

Chapter Six
Spreading Sin

God had cursed Satan, but he (was defiant and challenged God), saying, "I will ensnare a certain number of Your servants. I'll mislead them and urge them (to sin)." (*Qur'an* 4:118-119, Emerick translation)

And so it was that Iblis had used them to prove (the truth of) his notion (that he could corrupt humankind), and they followed him, save for a fragment who believed (in God). He had no (real) power over them. (He was only able to corrupt them) because We (had given him permission to try and deceive humanity if he could), in order that We could test (the sincerity) of the one who believes in the next life (and separate) him from the one who doubts in it. Your Lord is a guardian over all things. (*Qur'an* 34:20-21, Emerick translation)

So with deceit I assailed your wife and made you to be expelled through her from the joys of your bliss, as I have been expelled from my glory. (Life of Adam and Eve 16:3)[93]

INTRODUCTION

As the above passages make clear, having in his arrogance committed the first sin and having subsequently been cast down by God, Satan vowed to lead mankind astray. While Satan's whisperings tempt mankind to sin in various and sundry ways, one primary Satanic temptation is modeled on the motivation underlying Satan's own first sin, i.e., hubris and

---

[93] Johnson MD (2011), page 262.

arrogance. As such, as previously seen in chapter three, all three Abrahamic faiths condemn arrogance, and all three laud its opposite, i.e., humility and meekness. However, it is not just the individual arrogance of the common man that is condemned; both the *Bible* and the *Qur'an* specifically condemn individual arrogance in governmental leaders, as well as societal and national arrogance. Further, both enumerate multiple examples of past rulers and civilizations that were brought down and destroyed precisely because of their arrogance. In that regard, the *Qur'an* states the following.

> And so it was that We sent other (prophets) before you to the nations (of the world), and We inflicted (upon those nations) suffering and hardship so they could learn to be humble. So why didn't they learn to be humble when the suffering that We sent came upon them? On the contrary, their hearts became harder, and Satan made their deeds seem proper and good to them. (*Qur'an* 6:42-43, Emerick translation)

THE DESTRUCTION OF ARROGANT RULERS AND NATIONS

Some of the following events can be dated with some precision. However, dating the earliest of these events, especially dating the events not reported in Biblical accounts, is precarious at best. Nonetheless, the current author has attempted to provide a rough chronological ordering, starting with the earliest event and proceeding to the latest.

THE PEOPLE OF NOAH

Both the Torah's book of Genesis 6:11-8:19 and the *Qur'an* narrate the story of Noah and the flood. However, one difference between the Biblical and Qur'anic accounts of Noah's flood is the issue of why Noah's community earned divine wrath and destruction. While Genesis 6:11-13 attributes God's destruction of Noah's people due to their corruption and violence, the *Qur'an* specifically mentions the arrogance of Noah's people as one of the factors that contributed their destruction.

> We sent Noah to his people (with this instruction), "Warn your people before a painful punishment overtakes them."...(He was ignored, however, and in his despair he cried out to God), saying, "My Lord! I've called to my people through the night and through the day, but my invitation only (seems to) make them drift further away. Every time I've called to them so You could forgive them, they've stuck their fingers in their ears and wrapped themselves up in their cloaks, growing more stubborn and arrogant!"... On account of their sins, they were drowned (in the flood) and entered into a fire. They found no one to help them besides God. (*Qur'an* 71:1, 5-7, 25, Emerick translation)

THE PEOPLE OF 'AD

'Ad was a nation located in the southern part of Arabia, probably in the vicinity of modern Oman. Its major city was Iram, also known as Ubar, a city that was later swallowed up by the desert.[94] Dating 'Ad is a somewhat uncertain business, although Al-Tabari states that Hud, the prophet sent to 'Ad, lived in the eighth generation after Noah, which would place Hud just a couple of generations before Abraham.[95] Likewise, *Qur'an* 7:69 dates the destruction of 'Ad after the destruction of Noah's people, while *Qur'an* 40:27-31 says that 'Ad was destroyed prior to the Israelite exodus from Egypt under Moses and Aaron. While the destruction of 'Ad is not mentioned in the *Bible*, the *Qur'an* several times ties the destruction of 'Ad to its societal and national arrogance.

---

[94] (A) Emerick Y: (2000), page 237. (B) Clapp N (1998).
[95] Al-Tabari M (1987).

Spreading Sin

"You've had affliction and wrath from your Lord come upon you already," (Hud) replied, "(because of your arrogant rejection of the truth). Are you going to argue with me about the names that you've made up (for your idols), both you and your ancestors, without any permission from God? So wait and see, for I'll be waiting with you." Then We saved him and those who were with him through (an act of) mercy from Our Own self, and We cut out the roots of those who denied Our signs and who didn't believe. (*Qur'an* 7:71-72, Emerick translation)

And so that was the (people of) 'Ad. They renounced the signs of their Lord, disobeyed His messengers, and obeyed the commands of every arrogant enemy (of faith). They were pursued by a curse in this life, and on the Day of Assembly, (oh, how they'll be punished), for the 'Ad rejected their Lord, and so—away with the 'Ad, the people of Hūd! (*Qur'an* 11:59-60), Emerick translation)

As for the (people of) 'Ad, they acted arrogantly throughout the land against all right. They boasted, "Who is stronger in power than we are?" Didn't they see that God, the One Who created them, was infinitely mightier than they (could ever be)? They worked against Our signs with determination, so We sent a terrible sandstorm against them, causing many days of disaster, in order to give them a taste of the most degrading punishment this life can offer. The punishment of the next life will be even more degrading still, and they'll have no one to help them.(*Qur'an* 41:15-16, Emerick translation)

The People of Sodom

The story of the destruction of the Cities of the Plains, including

Sodom and Gomorrah, is told in some detail in Genesis 19. According to Biblical dating, this occurred during the 21st century BCE.[96] Likewise, the destruction of Sodom is referred to in several passages of the *Qur'an*. Both Genesis 19 and the Qur'anic accounts attribute Sodom's destruction to rampant and public homosexuality and homosexual rape. However, the Old Testament book of Ezekiel, one of the books of the Nevi'im, specifically lists pride and haughtiness as factors contributing to the destruction of Sodom. In referencing this passage from Ezekiel, the *Babylonian Talmud* also points a finger at pride and arrogance.

> This was the guilt of your sister Sodom: she and her daughters had pride, excess of food, and prosperous ease, but did not aid the poor and needy. They were haughty, and did abominable things before me; therefore I removed them when I saw it. (Ezekiel 16: 49-50, NRSV)

> And so it says, "As I live, says the Lord God, your sister Sodom and her daughters have not done as you and your daughters have done. Behold, this was the guilt of your sister Sodom: she and her daughters had pride, surfeit of food, and prosperous ease, but did not aid the poor and needy. They were haughty and did abominable things before me. Therefore I removed them when I saw it" (Ezekiel 16:48-50). (*Babylonian Talmud*, Tractate Sanhedrin, Neusner translation)

It is not just Ezekiel and the *Babylonian Talmud* that attribute Sodom and Gomorrah's destruction, at least in part, to arrogance. The same attribution is also found within two books in the Old Testament Apocrypha,

---

[96] Dirks JF (2002).

Spreading Sin

i.e., in Ecclesiasticus and III Maccabees.[97] With regard to the latter passage, the statement about Sodom being arrogant and being consumed by fire and sulfur is from a prayer offered up by Simon, the Jewish high priest.

> He did not spare the neighbors of Lot, whom he loathed on account of their arrogance. (Ecclesiasticus 16:8, NRSV)

> You consumed with fire and sulfur the people of Sodom who acted arrogantly, who were notorious for their vices; and you made them an example to those who should come afterward. (III Maccabees 2:5, NRSV)

How exactly were Sodom and Gomorrah destroyed? According to both Genesis 19:24-25 and III Maccabees 2:5, the cities were consumed with sulfur and fire that miraculously descended from Heaven.

THE PEOPLE OF THAMUD

The *Qur'an* describes the Thamud as being a people and nation that arose after the 'Ad[98] and before the Egypt of Moses and Aaron.[99] Qur'anic commentators have traditionally placed the Thamud in Al-Hijr, an area that lies in what is today southern Jordan and northern Saudi Arabia, and have dated the beginnings of the Thamud to about 2400 BCE.[100] In his monumental world history, Al-Tabari places the eponymous ancestor of the Thamud as being in the fourth generation after Noah and places Salih, the prophet sent to the Thamud, as being in the 12th generation after Noah.[101] While the Thamud are not mentioned by name in the *Bible*,

---

[97] While III Maccabees does not appear in the Protestant and Roman Catholic Old Testaments, it is included in the Greek Orthodox Old Testament. (A) Dirks JF (2011); (B) Dowd SE (1997). It is an example of Jewish apologetic literature and was probably first written in Greek circa 100 BCE in Alexandria, Egypt, by a Hellenized Jew. (A) Emmet CW (1971); (B) Dowd SE (1997); (C) Anderson H (2011a).
[98] *Qur'an* 7:73-74.
[99] *Qur'an* 40:27-31.
[100] Emerick Y: (2000), page 238.
[101] Al-Tabari M (1987).

several Qur'anic passages attribute the destruction of the Thamud to divine retribution brought on by the arrogance of the Thamud.

> We sent to the people of Thamud their brother Salih, and he said, "My people! Serve God! You have no other god than Him. Clear evidence has come to you from your Lord! This camel (that's been especially sanctified by) God is your sign, so leave her to graze on God's earth. Do her no harm, or you'll be seized with terrible punishment…
>
> The arrogant ones then said, "Well, we reject what you believe in!" Then they (cut the legs of the camel,) crippling her, and brazenly defied the order of their Lord. They (boasted about it) and said, "Salih! Bring on your threats, if you're really a messenger (of God)!"
>
> Then the mighty quake took them by surprise, and by morning they were left cowering in their homes. Salih (saw the damage and then) left them, saying, "My people! I conveyed to you the message that was sent to me from my Lord. I gave you good advice, but you had no love for advisors." (*Qur'an* 7:73, 76-79, Emerick translation)
>
> We sent to (the people of) Thamud their brother Salih. He said (to them), "My people! Serve God! You have no other god than Him…This camel (you see here is specially blessed) by God and is a sign for you. Therefore, leave her to graze on God's land and do her no harm, or a swift punishment will befall you."
>
> (Then the arrogant people among them) cut (her legs) and crippled her, so (Salih) told them, "Enjoy yourselves in your homes for the next three days, (after which you're going to be destroyed), and that's a promise that won't be proven false."

When Our command came, We saved Salih and those who believed along with him from the humiliation of that day through an act of Our Own mercy. Your Lord is Capable and Powerful! The mighty blast overtook the wrongdoers, and they lay cowering in their homes by the morning. (It looked) as if they had never lived or flourished there before! And so it was (their fate), for the Thamud rejected their Lord, and so—away with the Thamud! (*Qur'an* 11:61, 64-68, Emerick translation)

The (people of) Thamud rejected (this truth) in their audacity. The worst man among them rose up (to do an evil deed). Their messenger of God had told them, "This camel belongs to God, so let her drink (at the wells)." Then they called him an imposter, and (the wicked man) cruelly maimed her. So their Lord annihilated all of them equally for their crime, and He's not afraid of the consequences (of His actions). (*Qur'an* 91:11-15, Emerick translation)

THE PEOPLE OF MIDIAN

Midian was the fourth son of Abraham out of Keturah,[102] having been born circa 2015 BCE.[103] He was also the eponymous ancestor of the Midianites (the Madyan people) who lived in what is today northwestern Saudi Arabia. According to Genesis 25:4, Midian was the father of Ephah, Epher, Hanoch, Abida, and Eldaah. Al-Tabari variously list two other sons for Midian, i.e., Thabit and Mika'il, and gives two different genealogies for Shu'ayb, the prophet sent to the Midianites: (1) Midian, the father of Thabit, the father of 'Anqa, the father of Safyun, the father of Shu'ayb; (2) Midian, the father of Mika'il, the father of Shu'ayb.[104]

---

[102] (A) Genesis 25:1-2. (B) Jubilees 19:11-12.
[103] Dirks JF (2002)
[104] Al-Tabari (1987), page 143.

Some Qur'anic commentators have identified Shu'ayb with Moses' father-in-law, variously named in the *Bible* as: (1) Reuel in Exodus 2:15 b-22; (2) Jethro in Exodus 3:1; 4:18; and 18:1-12; (3) Hobab, the son of Reuel, in Numbers 10:29; and (4) Hobab, the Kenite, presumably a clan of the Midianites, in Judges 1:16. Further, if Al-Tabari is correct in listing Shu'ayb as being only five generations in descent from Abraham, this does compare favorably with Exodus 6:16-20 listing Moses as being only three generations in descent from Levi, the son of Jacob, the son of Isaac, the son of Abraham. However, the second genealogy given by Al-Tabari has Shu'ayb being only three generations in descent from Abraham. Further, *Qur'an* 7:85-103 clearly states that Moses was after the time of Shu'ayb and the destruction of Midian.[105] Still further, both the *Qur'an* and the *Bible* describe Moses' father-in-law as being an old desert shepherd, while the *Qur'an* describes Shu'ayb as living in a fixed settlement. In short, aside from the fact that Moses' father-in-law was a Midianite and that Moses and Shu'ayb may have been near contemporaries, there appears to be no real justification for identifying Shu'ayb with Moses' father-in-law.

Whatever the relationship between Shu'ayb and Moses' father-in-law, and whenever Shu'ayb might have lived, the *Qur'an* is quite explicit in attributing the destruction of the Midianite settlement to their arrogance.

> To (the people of) Madyan We sent their brother Shu'ayb, who said, "My people! Serve God! You have no other god than Him. Clear evidence has come to you from your Lord! So measure and balance honestly (in your trading activities), and don't withhold from people what they're owed. Don't cause disorder in the world after it's been made right. That will be to your good if you really have any faith…"

---

[105] In referring back to 7:85-93, *Qur'an* 7:103 reads: "Then after (their time) We sent Moses with Our signs to Pharaoh and his nobles…"

Spreading Sin

> The leaders of the arrogant faction among his people said, "Shu'ayb! We're going to drive you out of our settlement, both you and those who believe with you, unless all of you return to our traditions." …And then the earthquake took them without warning, and they lay cowering in their homes by morning.
>
> Those who denied Shu'ayb were reduced (in power), as much as if they never even had a vibrant civilization! It was those who denied Shu'ayb who were the losers! (*Qur'an* 7:85, 88, 91-92, Emerick translation)

The Egypt of Moses' Time

Both the *Bible* and the *Qur'an* state that the pharaoh who was Moses' antagonist and his Egyptian army were destroyed when the sea closed over them as they were pursuing the Israelites' flight from Egypt. In a short passage in the Torah, the destruction inflicted upon the Egyptians is said to have occurred because the Egyptians dealt arrogantly with the Israelites.

> Now I know that the Lord is greater than all gods, because he delivered the people from the Egyptians, when they dealt arrogantly with them. (Exodus 18:11, NRSV)

Likewise, the Old Testament Apocrypha states that Pharaoh and his Egyptian army were drowned by the hand of God because of their arrogance and boasting. The relevant passages are found in III Maccabees.

> You made known your mighty power by inflicting many and varied punishments on the audacious Pharaoh who had enslaved your holy people Israel. And when he pursued them with chariots and a mass of troops, you overwhelmed him in the depths of the sea… (III Maccabees 2:6-7, NRSV)

Pharaoh with his abundance of chariots, the former ruler of this Egypt, exalted with lawless insolence and boastful tongue, you destroyed together with his arrogant army by drowning them in the sea, manifesting the light of your mercy on the nation of Israel. (III Maccabees 6:4, NRSV)

Even more so than does the *Bible* and the Apocrypha, the *Qur'an* repeatedly stresses that the Egyptian army was drowned precisely because of the arrogance of Pharaoh and his minions. Further, the *Qur'an* attributes the plagues that beset Egypt before the Israelites began their flight from Egypt to the arrogance of the Egyptians. These numerous Qur'anic passages are quoted immediately below.

Then after them We sent Moses and Aaron with Our signs to Pharaoh and his nobles, but (the Egyptians) were an arrogant and wicked people…

And so it was that We took hold of Pharaoh and his people (and punished them) with years (of drought) and poor harvests so they could perhaps be reminded.

Whenever things got better, however, they said, "This is due to our own (diligent) efforts," though when stricken with hardship they said it was because of the evil omens of Moses and those who were with him. Their 'evil omens' were nothing more than their (own inventions), as far as God's view (was concerned,) but most of them didn't understand.

They said, "It doesn't matter what miracles you bring out in order to work your magic on us, (Moses,) for we're never going to believe in you!"

Spreading Sin

So We sent upon them a disastrous (flood), locusts, lice, frogs and a red-stained thing: signs that were self-explanatory, but they were arrogant, and they were a wicked people.

Every time a disaster would befall them, they would cry, "Moses! Call upon your Lord for us, invoking His promise to you. If you relieve us of this torment, then we'll truly believe in you and send the Children of Israel away with you."

Yet, every time We relieved them of the torment, after its due course was completed, they broke their word! So We got them back by drowning them in the sea, for they had (willfully) denied Our signs and were unconcerned about them. (*Qur'an* 10:75; 7:130-136, Emerick translation)

Then We sent Moses and his brother Aaron with Our signs and a clear mandate to Pharaoh and his nobles, but they acted arrogantly and were quite a conceited people. (Pharaoh and his nobles) said, "Should we believe in two mortal men who are just like us, especially since their people are our slaves!" So they denied them and were thus plunged into destruction. (*Qur'an* 23:45-48, Emerick translation)

When Our signs reached (the court of Pharaoh), so they might open their eyes, they said instead, "This is obviously magic!" Thus, they arrogantly scoffed at them (Moses and Aaron), even though they were convinced of them deep down in their souls. Then just see how we terminate the disobedient! (*Qur'an* 27:13-14, Emerick translation)

And so it was that before them we tested the people of Pharaoh. An honorable messenger (Moses) came to them, saying, "Release to me the servants of God, for I'm a trustworthy messenger (that's been sent) to you. Don't be arrogant against God, for I stand before you with the clear power (to command)."...(The Egyptians worked against him, however), so he called out to his Lord, "They're a wicked people!"

"Set out with My servants by night," (came the command,) "for you'll certainly be pursued. Leave the (parted) sea (that you'll have to cross through) alone, for (the Egyptian) forces that will (pursue you through it will) be drowned (when it collapses in on them)."

How many gardens and bubbling springs did they leave behind, and fields of grain, fine buildings and richness in which they delighted? That's (how it ended), and We let other peoples inherit (those things). Neither heaven above nor the earth shed a tear for them, nor were they given any chance to recover. (*Qur'an* 44: 17-19, 22-29, Emerick translation)

The above Qur'anic passages attest to Egypt being punished for its arrogance by a series of plagues followed by the destruction of Pharaoh and his Egyptian army as the sea closed in over them as they pursued the Israelites. However, the punishment Pharaoh and the Egyptians earned by their arrogance was not just confined to punishments in this life. As the following two Qur'anic passages illustrate, they will also be punished in the next life in the fires of Hell.

"Nobles!" Pharaoh said. "I don't know of any other god for you than myself. Haman! Fire up the (furnaces to make) bricks of clay, and build me a towering palace so I can climb up to the God of Moses. As for me, I think he's a liar!"

Spreading Sin

Against all right he was arrogant throughout the land, both he and his hordes. They never thought they would come back to Us! So we seized him, along with his hordes, and threw them into the sea! So just look at how wrongdoers are finished off!

We made (their conduct) the pinnacle of all invitations to the Fire, and they'll find no one to help them on the Day of Assembly. A curse will follow them in this world, and on the Day of Assembly they're going to be hideous (to behold, on account of how they're going to be disfigured). (*Qur'an* 28:38-42)

"I've called upon my Lord," Moses answered him, "(to protect me) from every arrogant (tyrant) who disbelieves in the Day of Account."...

"Haman!" Pharaoh commanded, "Build for me a tall tower so I can find a way—a way to reach up and enter into the heavens, so I'll be able to rise up to the God of Moses. As for me, I think he's a liar." Thus, Pharaoh's awful deeds seemed justified in his eyes. He was blocked from the path (of God), and whatever Pharaoh planned brought him nothing but ruin… and the reality of the (ultimate) punishment will soon surround the people of Pharaoh. They'll be brought in front of the Fire from morning to evening on the day when the Hour (of Judgment) will be established. "Admit the people of Pharaoh into the worst torment!"

Then they're going to argue with each other (as they're being marched into) the Fire. The weak-minded followers will say to their arrogant (leaders), "But we followed you (willingly)! Can't you take some of our burden of fire from us?"

"We're all in this together," the arrogant (leaders) will reply, "and God has indeed made judgments among (His) servants." Then those who are (plunged) into the Fire will plead with the wardens of Hell, "Call upon your Lord to ease the punishment for us - (at least) for a day!" (*Qur'an* 40:27, 36-37, 45-49, Emerick translation)

THE ANCIENT ISRAELITES

The Old Testament story of the Israelite Korah takes place as Moses was leading the Israelites through the wilderness following their escape from Egypt. According to the Torah's Numbers 16, Korah led a rebellion of Israelites against the authority of Moses and Aaron. Specifically, Korah and his group challenged God's teachings to Moses that certain sacred functions should be limited to Aaron and his priestly descendants. While the words "arrogance" and "pride" are not used in this Old Testament narrative, one can infer that Korah was acting quite arrogantly in challenging the leadership of Moses and Aaron. According to Numbers 16:31-35, in response to Korah's challenge to the leadership of Moses and Aaron, Korah and his household were swallowed up by the earth and descended into Hell.

The *Qur'an* also tells the story of Korah's destruction, but it attributes his destruction to his arrogance and his pride in his immense wealth. (While the Old Testament does not focus on Korah's wealth, the *Babylonian Talmud* states that Korah discovered one of the three treasures hidden by Joseph in Egypt and that Korah's wealth was so great that it took 300 mules to carry the keys to his treasure! [106])

---

[106] These statements about Korah's immense wealth may be found in Tractate Sanhedrin, chapter 11, and Tractate Pesahim, chapter 4, of the *Babylonian Talmud*.

Spreading Sin

Korah was from among Moses' people, but he behaved contemptuously towards his fellows. We bestowed upon him so much wealth that the very keys to (his treasure chests) weighed down a group of strong men.

One day his people told him, "Stop gloating, for God has no love for people who gloat."...However, he answered them, saying, "All this is mine from my own efforts and knowledge." Didn't he know that God had already destroyed before him many generations that were far stronger and wealthier than whatever he amassed? However, the wicked are not always made to answer for their sins (in this life).

So (Korah) strutted around among his people in all his finery... We made the earth open wide, and it swallowed both him and his entourage. He didn't have any supporters who could help him against God—he couldn't even help himself! (*Qur'an* 28:76, 78-79, 81, Emerick translation)

Several *Ahadith* also make mention of Korah and his arrogance, which was manifest in part by his habit of wearing clothes so long that they drug on the ground. In that regard, Prophet Muhammad said that God caused the earth to swallow up a person (identified as Korah in the *Musnad* of Ahmad ibn Hanbal and in the above Qur'anic passage), who was haughtily dragging his clothes on the ground.

'Abdullah ibn 'Umar narrated that God's Messenger said, "While a man was walking, dragging his dress with pride, he was caused to be swallowed by the earth and will go on sinking in it till the Day of Resurrection." (*Bukhari*, Volume 4, *Hadith* #692; see also Volume 7, *Hadith* #681)

Abu Huraira narrated that the Prophet said, "While a man was walking, clad in a two-piece garment and proud of himself with his hair well-combed, suddenly God made him sink into the earth, and he will go on sinking into it till the Day of Resurrection." (*Bukhari*, Volume 7, *Hadith* #680)

The Prophet once made mention of Korah, saying, "When a man from among the people who came before your time went out wearing two green garments, walking proudly and arrogantly, God commanded the earth to swallow him up, and he will remain sunk in the earth until the Day of Resurrection." (*Ahmad*)[107]

A second Qur'anic passage recounts the favors God bestowed upon the Israelites, including "clear directions" as to religion and conduct. Nonetheless, the Israelites split into "competing groups, due to arrogant jealousy." The passage ends by noting that God "will judge between them…on the Day of Judgment."

> And so it was that We granted the Children of Israel the Book (of scripture), the power to act, and the gift of prophethood. We also provided them with wholesome (food) and favored them above all others in the universe. We also gave them clear directions in all their affairs, but it was only after they received such knowledge that they fell into competing groups, due to arrogant jealousy among themselves. Their Lord will judge between them concerning these points of difference on the Day of Judgment. (*Qur'an* 45:16-17, Emerick translation)

---

[107] Emerick Y (2000), page 497.

Spreading Sin

The Northern Kingdom of Israel

The United Kingdom of Israel began in 1020 BCE under the kingship of Saul, and it continued throughout the kingships of David and Solomon. However, after the death of King Solomon in 931 or 930 BCE, the United Kingdom of Israel split into two smaller states. In the south, Rehoboam succeeded Solomon as the king of the Southern Kingdom of Judah, which is discussed in the next section of this chapter. In the north, Jeroboam became king of the Northern Kingdom of Israel.[108]

As the sequence of kings in the Northern Kingdom of Israel is likely to be unfamiliar to most readers, the following synopsis is offered. (1) Jeroboam's reign over the Northern Kingdom of Israel lasted for approximately 20 years, and he was then succeeded by Nadab in 910 or 909 BCE. (2) After one or two years as king, Nadab was killed and was succeeded by Baasha. (3) After ruling for 23 years, Baasha was succeeded by Elah in 886 or 885 BCE. (4) King Elah ruled for one year before being killed by Zimri, who ruled for only seven days. (5) Following Zimri, Omri and Tibni both claimed the throne of the Northern Kingdom of Israel. After four or five years of rival kingships, Omri became the sole king of the Northern Kingdom of Israel and built Samaria as Israel's capital city. (6) In 874 or 873 BCE, the infamous Ahab succeeded Omri as king. (7) Ahab was succeeded by Ahaziah in 853 BCE, and Jehoram succeeded Ahaziah just one year later in 852 BCE. (8) In 841 BCE, Jehoram was killed in a revolt led by Jehu, who then became king, although he was a vassal to and paid tribute to King Shalmaneser III of Assyria. (9) In 814 or 813 BCE, Jehu was succeeded by Jehoahaz. (10) Jehoahaz then ruled for approximately 32 years before dying and being succeeded by Jeroboam II in 782 or 781 BCE. (11) Then in 753 BCE, Zechariah succeeded Jeroboam II,

---
[108] Duncan GB (1971).

but his reign lasted only one year before he was killed. (12) Shallum then usurped the throne, but he ruled only one month before being overthrown by Menahem, who later paid tribute to King Tiglathpileser III of Assyria. (13) Menahem was then succeeded by Pekahiah in 742 or 741 BCE. (14) Two years later, Pekahiah was killed, and the throne was usurped by Pekah. (15) In 732 or 731 BCE, Pekah was killed, and Hoshea claimed the throne as an Assyrian vassal. (16) However, after seven years serving as a vassal king under the Assyrians, Hoshea revolted against Assyrian suzerainty in 725 or 724 BCE. King Shalmaneser V of Assyria then invaded the Northern Kingdom of Israel and laid siege to the capital city of Samaria. Two years later, Samaria fell to the Assyrians, and many Israelites were sent into exile in Assyria. At that point, the Northern Kingdom of Israel was no more.[109]

Jeroboam, the very first king of the Northern Kingdom of Israel, is said in the *Babylonian Talmud* to have been so arrogant that he introduced idolatry into his kingdom rather than practice humility before God at the Temple of Solomon in Jerusalem. The passage quoted below further attests to the fact that it was this arrogance that drove King Jeroboam "out of the world."

> The arrogance that characterized Jeroboam is what drove him out of the world. For it is said, "Now Jeroboam said in his heart, 'Now shall the kingdom return to the house of David. If this people go up to sacrifice in the house of the Lord at Jerusalem, then shall the heart of this people turn to their Lord, even to Rehoboam, king of Judah, and they shall kill me and go again to Rehoboam, king of Judah' (1Ki. 12:27-26). He said, 'We have a tradition that no one may sit down in the Temple courtyard except kings of

---

[109] Duncan GB (1971).

the house of Judah alone. When the people see that Rehoboam is sitting down and I am standing, they will think that he is king, and I am merely a servant. But if I sit down, I shall be in the position of rebelling against the monarchy, and they will kill me and follow.' Forthwith: wherefore the king took counsel and made two calves of gold and said to them, 'It is too much for you to go up to Jerusalem. Behold your gods, O Israel, who brought you up out of the land of Egypt,' and he put one in Beth El and the other he put in Dan (I Kings 12:28)." (*Babylonian Talmud*, Tractate Sanhedrin, Neusner translation)

What was the divine punishment that befell Jeroboam for his idolatry and arrogance? According to I Kings 14:1-18, Jeroboam's son Abijah fell sick and died. Additionally, I Kings 15:25-30 states that upon Jeroboam's death, his son Nadab succeeded to the throne, but he ruled only one or two years before being killed in a coup led by Baasha. Upon seizing the throne, Baasha then had all the members of Jeroboam's family killed. In the final analysis, the complete extermination of Jeroboam and his family was the punishment paid by Jeroboam's for his arrogance.

More general condemnations of the arrogance of the Northern Kingdom of Israel can be found in the Old Testament. For example, the Nevi'im section of the Old Testament lists several notables who prophesized the Northern Kingdom of Israel would fall because of its pride and arrogance. Included among these notables were Hosea, Amos, and Isaiah. In the passage quoted below from Amos, the referenced city was Samaria, the capital of the Northern Kingdom of Israel. The quotation from Isaiah specifically refers to Samaria by name and to the tribe of Ephraim, one of the two tribes descending from Joseph, the son of Jacob, both of which occupied portions of the Northern Kingdom of Israel. As such, this passage can clearly be seen as a prophesized destruction of the Northern

Kingdom of Israel due to its pride and arrogance.

> It was I who fed you in the wilderness, in the land of drought. When I fed them, they were satisfied; they were satisfied, and their heart was proud; therefore they forgot me. So I will become like a lion to them, like a leopard I will lurk beside the way. I will fall upon them like a bear robbed of her cubs, and will tear open the covering of their heart; there I will devour them like a lion, as a wild animal would mangle them. I will destroy you, O Israel… (Hosea 13:5-9, NRSV)

> The Lord God has sworn by himself (says the Lord, the God of hosts): I abhor the pride of Jacob and hate his strongholds; and I will deliver up the city and all that is in it. (Amos 6:8, NRSV)

> The Lord sent a word against Jacob, and it fell on Israel; and all the people knew it—Ephraim and the inhabitants of Samaria—but in pride and arrogance of heart they said: "The bricks have fallen, but we will build with dressed stones; the sycamores have been cut down, but we will put cedars in their place." So the Lord raised adversaries against them, and stirred up their enemies, the Arameans on the east and the Philistines on the west, and they devoured Israel with open mouth. For all this his anger has not turned away; his hand is stretched out still. (Isaiah 9:8-12, NRSV)

Despite the fact that the passage from Isaiah predicts the destruction of the Northern Kingdom of Israel by the Arameans and Philistines, they were not the protagonists that annihilated Israel. As noted previously, the prophesized destruction of the Northern Kingdom of Israel was accomplished in 723-722 BCE by the invasion of Assyrian military forces.

Assyria

Assyria was a kingdom in northern Mesopotamia, spanning an area that includes what is now northern Iraq and southeastern Turkey. During most of the second millennium BCE, Assyria was a vassal of either Babylonia in southern Mesopotamia or of the Mitanni kingdom. Beginning in the 14th century BCE, Assyria became an independent kingdom. Over the next several centuries, Assyria's power and influence waxed and waned a few times. However, during the eighth and seventh centuries BCE, Assyria became the major power in the Middle East, ruling from the borders of Egypt, through the Fertile Crescent, and down to the Persian Gulf. It was this Assyria that wiped out the Northern Kingdom of Israel.[110]

However, during its long rule over the Fertile Crescent, Assyria was not without its defeats. For example, in 701 BCE, King Sennacherib of Assyria (ruled 705/04-681 BCE) began to lay siege to Jerusalem, the capital city of the Southern Kingdom of Judah. In response, King Hezekiah of Judah prayed for deliverance, and God promised that he would defeat Sennacherib and his arrogance. In the books of Isaiah and II Kings in the Old Testament Nevi'im and in the book of III Maccabees in the Old Testament Apocrypha, Sennacherib's defeat and assassination are attributed to his pride and arrogance.

> Then Isaiah son of Amoz sent to Hezekiah, saying: "Thus says the Lord, the God of Israel: Because you have prayed to me concerning King Sennacherib of Assyria, this is the word that the Lord has spoken concerning him…Because you have raged against me and your arrogance has come to my ears, I will put my hook in your nose and my bit in your mouth; I will turn you back on the way by which you came." (Isaiah 37:21-22, 29, NRSV)

---

[110] --- (2003a).

Then Isaiah son of Amoz sent to Hezekiah, saying, "Thus says the Lord, the God of Israel: I have heard your prayer to me about King Sennacherib of Assyria. This is the word that the Lord has spoken concerning him...Because you have raged against me and your arrogance has come to my ears, I will put my hook in your nose and my bit in your mouth; I will turn you back on the way by which you came. (II Kings 19:20-21 & 28, NRSV)

Sennacherib exulting in his countless forces, oppressive king of the Assyrians, who had already gained control of the whole world by the spear and was lifted up against your holy city, speaking grievous words with boasting and insolence, you, O Lord, broke in pieces, showing your power to many nations. (III Maccabees 6:4-5, NRSV)

The exact nature of this defeat of the Assyrians is reported in Isaiah 37:36-38, II Kings 19:35-37, II Chronicles 32:20-21, and I Maccabees 7:40-41 where it is variously stated that God sent an angel to lay waste to the Assyrians and that 185,000 Assyrian soldiers were killed. Sennacherib then retreated back to his capital city of Nineveh where he was assassinated by two of his sons.

The defeat of King Sennacherib and his Assyrian army is also alluded to in the book of Judith[111] in the Old Testament Apocrypha, although King Sennacherib is not mentioned by name. As noted in the passage quoted below, Judith prayed to God for Assyria's destruction, noting that Assyria was puffed up with conceited arrogance, priding itself in its military might.

---

[111] Judith was probably written by a Palestinian Jew who belonged to the Pharisaic party of Judaism. Its date of composition is likely to have been in the second century BCE, circa 150 BCE. Its original language was probably Hebrew, although the oldest existing text of Judith is in Greek. (A) Richardson HN (1971b); (B) Cowley AE (1971).

Spreading Sin

> Then Judith prostrated herself, put ashes on her head, and uncovered the sackcloth she was wearing. At the very time when the evening incense was being offered in the house of God in Jerusalem, Judith cried out to the Lord with a loud voice, and said…"Here now are the Assyrians, a greatly increased force, priding themselves in their horses and riders, boasting in the strength of their foot soldiers, and trusting in shield and spear, in bow and sling. They do not know that you are the Lord who crushes wars; the Lord is your name. Break their strength by your might, and bring down their power in your anger; for they intend to defile your sanctuary, and to pollute the tabernacle where your glorious name resides, and to break off the horns of your altar with the sword. Look at their pride, and send your wrath upon their heads. Give to me, a widow, the strong hand to do what I plan. By the deceit of my lips strike down the slave with the prince and the prince with his servant; crush their arrogance by the hand of a woman." (Judith 9:1, 7-10, NRSV)

Despite King Sennacherib's defeat and assassination, Assyria continued to rule over much of the Fertile Crescent and Middle East for many years. However, Ashurbanipal, Assyria's last strong king, died in 627 BCE, and Assyria's fortunes appear to have markedly declined after that. Little is known about Assyria post Ashurbanipal other than the fact that Assyria was destroyed by a Babylonian (Chaldean)-Median coalition in 612-609 BCE.[112] What led to the eventual destruction of Assyria? During its glory years, the pride and arrogance of Assyria began to know no bounds. As such, the Biblical books of Isaiah and Zechariah in the Nevi'im prophesized the final fall and destruction of Assyria that took place at the hands of the Babylonians.

---

[112] (A) Duncan GB (1971); (B) --- (2003a).

When the Lord has finished all his work on Mount Zion and on Jerusalem, he will punish the arrogant boasting of the king of Assyria and his haughty pride. (Isaiah 10:12, NRSV)

The pride of Assyria shall be laid low… (Zechariah 10:11)

THE PHILISTINES

The Philistines were a seafaring people of Aegean origin, who were quite likely originally from Crete. Late in the 13th century BCE they successfully raided and ravaged what is today Turkey, Cyprus, and Syria. Shortly thereafter, about 1190 BCE, they invaded Egypt but were repulsed. They then occupied the coastline of Palestine and established the five city-states of Gaza, Ashkelon, Ashdod, Gath, and Ekron. From that vantage point, they were frequently in conflict with the Israelites and, at times, were able to occupy part of the hill country in the south of Palestine. They were finally defeated in the late 11th century or early 10th century BCE by King David of Israel. However, after Israel split into the Northern Kingdom of Israel and the Southern Kingdom of Judah, the Philistines regained their independence and engaged in a series of military skirmishes with both kingdoms. Beginning in the early part of the seventh century BCE, the Philistines became vassals to a series of foreign rulers, including the Assyrians, the Egyptians, the Babylonians, the Persians, the Greeks, and the Romans.[113]

The end of Philistine pride is foretold in Zechariah 9:5-6, and the destruction or anguish of four of the five Philistine city-states is directly mentioned. While Zechariah is known to have prophesized circa 520 BCE, Biblical scholars are in agreement that chapters 9-14 of Zechariah[114] were not written by Zechariah. Thus, the actual dating of the passage quoted below is unknown, and one cannot identify the punishment inflicted

---

[113] --- (2003f).
[114] Carstensen RN (1971).

on the Philistines with any specific historical event.

> Ashkelon shall see it and be afraid; Gaza too, and shall writhe in anguish; Ekron also, because its hopes are withered. The king shall perish from Gaza; Ashkelon shall be uninhabited; a mongrel people shall settle in Ashdod, and I will make an end of the pride of Philistia. (Zechariah 9:5-6, NRSV)

SIXTH-CENTURY THROUGH FOURTH-CENTURY BCE EGYPT

In 609 BCE, Pharaoh Neco of Egypt deposed King Jehoahaz of the Southern Kingdom of Judah, replaced Jehoahaz with Jehoiakim as an Egyptian vassal, and was allying with the Assyrians against the Babylonians in Palestine. Approximately four years later, Nebuchadrezzar II of Babylonia defeated Pharaoh Neco, his Egyptian army, and the depleted Assyrian forces at Carchemish. At that point, the Southern Kingdom of Judah became a vassal of Babylonia. Three years after that, in 601 BCE, Babylonian forces experienced heavy losses in an attempt to invade Egypt. Emboldened by this Babylonian defeat, King Jehoiakim of Judah refused to pay the tribute that was due to Babylonia from Judah. In response, Nebuchadrezzar II and his Babylonian army laid siege to Jerusalem in 598/97 BCE, about the time Jehoiachin succeeded Johoiakim as king of Judah. On March 16, 597 BCE, Jerusalem fell to the Babylonian army, and Babylonia made Zedekiah its regent over Judah. In 589 BCE, under the influence of Egyptian sympathizers, Zedekiah revolted against Babylonian rule and was aided by Pharaoh Hophra of Egypt. In response, Nebuchadrezzar II and his Babylonian forces again invaded Judah, defeated the Egyptian forces of Pharaoh Hophra in 588 BCE, and laid waste to Jerusalem in 586 BCE.[115]

---

[115] Duncan GB (1971).

The First Sin: Jewish, Christian, and Islamic Perspectives

The above events serve as the historical context for the following passage from the Biblical book of Ezekiel, in which it is prophesized that God would use Nebuchadrezzar II and his Babylonian army so that "Egypt shall fall, and its proud might shall come down." The extent of this prophesized destruction was predicted to extend from Migdol in the northern delta region of Egypt to Syene near the Egyptian-Ethiopian border, near to modern Aswan.[116]

> Thus says the Lord: Those who support Egypt shall fall, and its proud might shall come down; from Migdol to Syene they shall fall within it by the sword, says the Lord God…Thus says the Lord God: I will put an end to the hordes of Egypt, by the hand of King Nebuchadrezzar of Babylon. He and his people with him, the most terrible of the nations, shall be brought in to destroy the land; and they shall draw their swords against Egypt, and fill the land with the slain…At Tehaphnehes the day shall be dark, when I break there the dominion of Egypt, and its proud might shall come to an end; the city shall be covered by a cloud, and its daughter-towns shall go into captivity. Thus I will execute acts of judgment on Egypt. Then they shall know that I am the Lord. (Ezekiel 30:6, 10-11, 18-19, NRSV)

While Nebuchadrezzar II did defeat the Egyptian forces of Pharaoh Hophra in 588 BCE, there was no wholesale destruction of Egypt by Babylonia. In fact, Egypt remained independent and free from Babylonian rule. It was not until 525 BCE that Egypt was finally conquered, not by the Babylonians, but by the Persian army of Cambyses. (The Persians under the command of King Cyrus the Great had previously invaded and defeated Babylonia in 539 BCE, and Cambyses had succeeded Cyrus as king in 530 BCE.)[117]

---

[116] Brownlee WH (1971).
[117] (A) Duncan GB (1971); (B) Brownlee WH (1971).

The Southern Kingdom of Judah

As noted above, following the death of King Solomon circa 931 BCE, the Kingdom of Israel split into two separate and independent entities. The Northern Kingdom of Israel was initially ruled by Jeroboam, while Rehoboam began his rule as king in the Southern Kingdom of Judah. As many readers may be unfamiliar with the various kings of the Southern Kingdom of Judah, the years of their reign, and the events surrounding their rule, Table #1 is presented below. This table presents a listing of the various kings of the Southern Kingdom of Judah between the time of the death of King Solomon in the 10th century BCE and the final destruction of the Southern Kingdom of Judah by the Babylonians in 586 BCE.

THE KINGS OF THE SOUTHERN KINGDOM OF JUDAH

KING	RULED	MISC.
Rehoboam	931/30-913 BCE	
Abijam	913-911/10 BCE	
Asa	911/10-870/69 BCE	
Jehoshaphat	873/72-848 BCE	Was briefly a co-regent with Asa.
Jehoram	854/53-841 BCE.	Initially, he was co-regent with Jehoshaphat.
Ahaziah	841 BCE	Killed while revolting against Assyria.
Athaliah	841-835 BCE	Killed.
Jehoash	835-796 BCE	Assassinated.
Amaziah	796-792/91 BCE	Captured in war between Israel and Judah.
Azariah	792/91-740/39 BCE	Contracts leprosy in 750 BCE.
Amaziah	782/81-767 BCE	Freed and returns as co-regent; assassinated.
Jotham	750-732/31 BCE	Co-regent with Ahaz late in life.

KING	RULED	MISC.
Ahaz	735-716/15 BCE	
Hezekiah	716/15-687/86 BCE	Co-regent with Manasseh later in life.
Manasseh	697/96-643/42 BCE	
Amon	643/42-641/40 BCE	
Josiah	641/40-609 BCE	Killed.
Jehoahaz	609 BCE	Deposed by Pharaoh Neco of Egypt.
Jehoiakim	609-598/97 BCE	
Jehoiachin	598/97-597 BCE	Captured and exiled by Babylonians.
Zedekiah	597-586 BCE	Made regent by Babylonians, revolted against them in 589 BCE, and captured by the Babylonians in 586 BCE.

Within the pages of the Old Testament, numerous passages predict the destruction of the Southern Kingdom of Judah, as well as several of its kings, due to the sin of prideful arrogance. With regard to individual kings being brought low because of their haughtiness and self-conceit, the following passage from II Chronicles, one of the books of the Old Testament Ketuvim, tells of the destruction of King Azariah (aka Uzziah) due to his wanton pride. Of note, King Azariah ruled the Southern Kingdom of Judah from 792/91-740/39 BCE.

> Then all the people of Judah took Uzziah, who was sixteen years old, and made him king to succeed his father Amaziah…But when he had become strong he grew proud, to his destruction. For he was false to the Lord his God, and entered the temple of the Lord to make offering on the altar of incense. (II Chronicles 26:1 & 16, NRSV)

Spreading Sin

As noted in the above passage from II Chronicles, King Azariah's arrogance was such that he usurped a role reserved exclusively for the priests and performed his own offering on the altar of incense in the Temple of Solomon! What was the destruction inflicted on King Azariah for his arrogance and pride? In 750 BCE, King Azariah came down with leprosy, a most horrifying and disfiguring disease. Only about 10 years later, he was dead.

A second king of the Southern Kingdom of Judah who suffered divine punishment for his arrogance was King Hezekiah. Hezekiah ruled over Judah from 716/15-687/86 BCE. Despite having had his prayers answered for a recovery from illness and for the Assyrian army's defeat as it was besieging Jerusalem in 701 BCE, Hezekiah became proud and arrogant. Due to his arrogance, Hezekiah and his kingdom are said to have suffered the wrath of God. However, unlike other arrogant rulers, Hezekiah then humbled himself before God, and the wrath of God was subsequently lifted from Hezekiah and from the Southern Kingdom of Judah, demonstrating that sincere repentance for sinful pride and arrogance is accepted by God.

> In those days Hezekiah became sick and was at the point of death. He prayed to the Lord, and he answered him and gave him a sign. But Hezekiah did not respond according to the benefit done to him, for his heart was proud. Therefore wrath came upon him and upon Judah and Jerusalem. Then Hezekiah humbled himself for the pride of his heart, both he and the inhabitants of Jerusalem, so that the wrath of the Lord did not come upon them in the days of Hezekiah. (II Chronicles 32:24-26, NRSV)

A second passage dealing with King Hezekiah and the Southern Kingdom of Judah may be found in Isaiah. That this passage deals with a judgment against the Southern Kingdom of Judah can be seen by the reference to Jerusalem, which was the capital city of the Southern Kingdom of Judah. The "nation far away" mentioned in verse 26 apparently refers to the Assyrian invasion of Judah by Sennacherib in 701 BCE during the reign of King Hezekiah of Judah.[118]

> Therefore Sheol has enlarged its appetite and opened its mouth beyond measure; the nobility of Jerusalem and her multitude go down, her throng and all who exult in her. People are bowed down, everyone is brought low, and the eyes of the haughty are humbled…He will raise a signal for a nation far away, and whistle for a people at the ends of the earth; here they come, swiftly, speedily! None of them is weary, none stumbles, none slumbers or sleeps, not a loincloth is loose, not a sandal-thong broken; their arrows are sharp, all their bows bent, their horses' hoofs seem like flint, and their wheels like the whirlwind. Their roaring is like a lion, like young lions they roar; they growl and seize their prey, they carry it off, and no one can rescue. They will roar over it on that day, like the roaring of the sea. And if one look to the land—only darkness and distress; and the light grows dark with clouds. (Isaiah 5:14-15, 26-30, NRSV)

King Amon ruled Judah for just two years (643/42-641/40). As documented in II Chronicles, King Amon practiced idolatry and refused to humble himself before God. As a result of his idolatry and arrogant refusal to practice humility before God, he was assassinated by his own servants in his house.

> Amon was twenty-two years old when he began to reign; he reigned two years in Jerusalem. He did what was evil in the sight

---

[118] Ackroyd PR (1971).

of the Lord, as his father Manasseh had done. Amon sacrificed to all the images that his father Manasseh had made, and served them. He did not humble himself before the Lord, as his father Manasseh had humbled himself, but this Amon incurred more and more guilt. His servants conspired against him and killed him in his house. (II Chronicles 33:21-24, NRSV)

The Southern Kingdom of Judah was finally and utterly destroyed by the Babylonians. With regard to the punishment of the Kingdom of Judah by the Babylonians, this event can be precisely dated. Babylonian military forces under the command of Nebuchadrezzar II captured Palestine from Egypt in 605 BCE, the Kingdom of Judah having been a vassal state to Egypt. At that point, the Kingdom of Judah became a vassal to Babylonia. A few months later, Nebuchadrezzar II became king of Babylonia. In 601 BCE, Babylonia sustained heavy losses in an attempt to invade Egypt. Thinking Babylonia to be seriously weakened, in his arrogance, King Jehoiakim of the Kingdom of Judah began to withhold tribute from Babylonia. Circa 598/97 BCE, Jehoiakim was succeeded as king of Judah by Jehoiachin. About the same time, Nebuchadrezzar II responded to Judah's arrogant refusal to pay tribute by besieging Jerusalem, which eventually fell on March 16, 597 BCE. Many of Judah's leading citizens were exiled to Babylonia, and Nebuchadrezzar II installed Zedekiah as the puppet ruler of Judah.[119]

However, the above scenario constituted only the first stage in the final destruction of the Southern Kingdom of Judah due to its conceited arrogance. In 589 BCE, the pro-Egyptian block in Judah forced Zedekiah to revolt against Babylonia. Thus, on January 15, 588 BCE, Nebuchadrezzar II again set siege to Jerusalem. This initial siege was

---

[119] Duncan GB (1971).

unsuccessful, as Nebuchadrezzar II was forced to interrupt his siege in order to drive back an attempted invasion of Palestine by Pharaoh Hophra of Egypt. After returning his attention to Jerusalem, Nebuchadrezzar II finally broke through the walls of Jerusalem on July 18, 586 BCE. On August 14 or 17 of that same year, the Babylonians began the destruction of Jerusalem and its Temple of Solomon, and many more Jews were sent into exile in Babylonia.[120]

As noted in the following passage from the Old Testament Ketuvim, it was the arrogance of King Zedekiah of Judah that contributed to the final and utter destruction of Judah and its capital of Jerusalem by the Babylonians (a.k.a. Chaldeans).

> Zedekiah was twenty-one years old when he began to reign; he reigned eleven years in Jerusalem. He did what was evil in the sight of the Lord his God. He did not humble himself before the prophet Jeremiah who spoke from the mouth of the Lord. He also rebelled against King Nebuchadnezzar...The Lord, the God of their ancestors, sent persistently to them by his messengers, because he had compassion on his people and on his dwelling place; but they kept mocking the messengers of God, despising his words, and scoffing at his prophets, until the wrath of the Lord against his people became so great that there was no remedy. Therefore he brought up against them the king of the Chaldeans, who killed their youths with the sword in the house of their sanctuary, and had no compassion on young man or young woman, the aged or the feeble; he gave them all into his hand. All the vessels of the house of God, large and small, and the treasures of the house of the Lord, and the treasures of the king and of his officials, all these he brought to Babylon. They burned the house

---

[120] Duncan GB (1971).

of God, broke down the wall of Jerusalem, burned all its palaces with fire, and destroyed all its precious vessels. He took into exile in Babylon those who had escaped from the sword, and they became servants to him and to his sons until the establishment of the kingdom of Persia… (II Chronicles 36:11-13, 15-20 NRSV)

Numerous other passages from the Old Testament Nevi'im attribute the fall and destruction of the Southern Kingdom of Judah to the arrogance of the kingdom and its rulers. For example, the first passage quoted below is taken from a long judgment that was pronounced on arrogance and that was directed at the Southern Kingdom of Judah. The second passage from Isaiah that is quoted below can be seen to be talking about the Southern Kingdom of Judah in that the daughters of Zion (a.k.a. Judah) are specifically mentioned. In addition, the following passage from Jeremiah is taken from a rather long condemnation of the Israelites of the Southern Kingdom of Judah. Across all three passages, arrogance, haughtiness, and pride are roundly condemned, and the passages warn that God will humble and put an end to nations and peoples who have such character traits.

> The haughty eyes of people shall be brought low, and the pride of everyone shall be humbled; and the Lord alone will be exalted on that day. For the Lord of hosts has a day against all that is proud and lofty, against all that is lifted up and high…The haughtiness of people shall be humbled, and the pride of everyone shall be brought low; and the Lord alone will be exalted on that day. (Isaiah 2:11-12 & 17, NRSV)

> The Lord said: Because the daughters of Zion are haughty and walk with outstretched necks, glancing wantonly with their eyes, mincing along as they go, tinkling with their feet; the Lord will afflict with scabs the heads of the daughters of Zion, and the Lord

will lay bare their secret parts. (Isaiah 3:16-17, NRSV)

Thus says the Lord: Just so I will ruin the pride of Judah and the great pride of Jerusalem….Hear and give ear; do not be haughty, for the Lord has spoken. (Jeremiah 13:9, 15, NRSV)

Additional condemnation of the arrogance and pride of the Southern Kingdom of Judah is found in Ezekiel, another of the books of the Nevi'im. The following passage from Ezekiel is particularly striking in that it is God Himself Who is reportedly vowing to strike down the arrogance of the strong. God's statement is specifically directed at the Israelites in the Southern Kingdom of Judah, and the "worst of the nations" that will destroy the Kingdom of Judah is Babylonia.

Thus says the Lord God…I will bring the worst of the nations to take possession of their houses. I will put an end to the arrogance of the strong, and their holy places shall be profaned…I will make the land a desolation and a waste, and its proud might shall come to an end; and the mountains of Israel shall be so desolate that no one will pass through. (Ezekiel 7:5 & 24b; 33:28, NRSV)

Two further passages from the Old Testament Nevi'im prophesize the fall of the Southern Kingdom of Judah. The first is from a section of Micah that dates to the late eighth century BCE.[121] The second is from Zephaniah and probably dates to the late seventh century BCE.[122]

Therefore thus says the Lord: Now, I am devising against this family an evil from which you cannot remove your necks; and you shall not walk haughtily, for it will be an evil time. (Micah 2:3, NRSV)

---

[121] Dahlberg DT (1971).
[122] Duncan GB (1971).

Spreading Sin

> Therefore wait for me, says the Lord...On that day you shall not be put to shame because of all the deeds by which you have rebelled against me; for then I will remove from your midst your proudly exultant ones, and you shall no longer be haughty in my holy mountain. For I will leave in the midst of you a people humble and lowly. They shall seek refuge in the name of the Lord— (Zephaniah 3:8, 11-12, NRSV)

It is not just the *Bible* that attributes the utter destruction of the Southern Kingdom of Judah to its prideful arrogance. The *Qur'an* specifically states that the Southern Kingdom of Judah was destroyed because of its conceited arrogance and that Jerusalem was again destroyed in 70 CE during the Judaean revolt against the Roman Empire during the years 66-73 CE. As noted previously, the first such destruction was accomplished at the hands of the Babylonians, while the second was inflicted by the Romans.

> We warned the Children of Israel in (their) scripture that they would twice cause corruption in the earth and be filled with conceited arrogance, (and thus they would be punished twice). When the first warning came to pass, We sent Our servants, (the Babylonians) against you, and they were greatly skilled in warfare. They rampaged through every part of your homes, and thus it was a warning fulfilled!
>
> ...Then later, when the second warning came to pass, (after you had become disobedient once more), your faces were framed in disgrace as (the Romans) entered into your temple of prayer, even as (the Babylonians) had done so (long before), and they destroyed whatever they laid their hands on. (*Qur'an* 17:4-5, 7, Emerick translation)

Moab

The Moabites were an ancient people who descended from Moab, their eponymous ancestor. In turn, Moab was the son of Lot, the nephew of Abraham.[123] The Moabites were primarily located east of the Dead Sea in what is now west-central Jordan. The Moab kingdom reached its peak in the 10th and ninth centuries BCE, during which time it lost and then regained land from the Northern Kingdom of Israel. By the late eighth century BCE, Moab had been reduced to being an Assyrian vassal state.[124]

Despite being reduced to a mere vassal, the Biblical books of Isaiah, Jeremiah, and Zephaniah document Moab's continuing arrogance, an arrogance that all three Biblical books prophesized would lead to Moab's eventual destruction. That destruction finally occurred in 582 BCE when the Babylonians conquered Moab and deleted it from the pages of subsequent history.

> We have heard of the pride of Moab—how proud he is!—of his arrogance, his pride, and his insolence; his boasts are false. Therefore let Moab wail, let everyone wail for Moab. Mourn, utterly stricken, for the raisin cakes of Kir-hareseth. (Isaiah 16: 6-7, NRSV)

> For the hand of the Lord will rest on this mountain. The Moabites shall be trodden down in their place as straw is trodden down in a dung-pit. Though they spread out their hands in the midst of it, as swimmers spread out their hands to swim, their pride will be laid low despite the struggle of their hands. (Isaiah 25:10-11, NRSV)

> We have heard of the pride of Moab—he is very proud—of his loftiness, his pride, and his arrogance, and the haughtiness of his

---
[123] Genesis 19:30-38.
[124] --- (2003b)

heart. I myself know his insolence, says the Lord; his boasts are false, his deeds are false. Therefore I wail for Moab; I cry out for all Moab; for the people of Kir-heres I mourn...Moab shall be destroyed as a people, because he magnified himself against the Lord. Terror, pit, and trap are before you, O inhabitants of Moab! says the Lord. Everyone who flees from the terror shall fall into the pit, and everyone who climbs out of the pit shall be caught in the trap. For I will bring these things upon Moab in the year of their punishment, says the Lord. (Jeremiah 48:29-31, 42-44, NRSV)

I have heard the taunts of Moab and the revilings of the Ammonites, how they have taunted my people and made boasts against their territory. Therefore, as I live, says the Lord of hosts, the God of Israel, Moab shall become like Sodom and the Ammonites like Gomorrah, a land possessed by nettles and salt pits, and a waste forever. The remnant of my people shall plunder them, and the survivors of my nation shall possess them. This shall be their lot in return for their pride, because they scoffed and boasted against the people of the Lord of hosts. (Zephaniah 2: 8-10, NRSV)

Tyre

Tyre was a Phoenician city-state located on an island in the Mediterranean Sea just off the coast of what is now southern Lebanon. From about 2000 BCE onwards, it served as a major Phoenician seaport. By the 14th century BCE, it was a vassal to Egypt, although it later gained its independence and ruled over all of Phoenicia at various times. During the eighth and seventh centuries BCE, it was subject to Assyria. However, between 585 and 573 BCE, it withstood a major siege by Nebuchadrezzar II and the Babylonian army. Nonetheless, between 538 and 332 BCE, it was once again a vassal state, being subject to the kings of Persia. In 332 BCE, Tyre fell to the forces of Alexander the Great, at which time 10,000 of its residents were put to death and another 30,000 were sold into slavery. Shortly thereafter until falling under Seleucid rule in 200 BCE, Tyre was under the rule of Ptolemaic Egypt. In 64 BCE, Tyre fell to Roman rule.[125]

The prophesized destruction of Tyre due to the arrogance of its king, probably Ithbaal II, is directly stated in a passage in the Biblical book of Ezekiel. Ezekiel prophesized in the sixth century BCE, so the destruction promised in the following Biblical passage may well refer to Tyre falling to the Persian kingdom later in the sixth century BCE.

> Mortal, say to the prince of Tyre, Thus says the Lord God: Because your heart is proud and you have said, "I am a god; I sit in the seat of the gods, in the heart of the seas,"… yet you are but a mortal, and no god, though you compare your mind with the mind of a god… By your great wisdom in trade you have increased your wealth, and your heart has become proud in your wealth. Therefore thus says the Lord God: Because you compare your mind with the mind of a god, therefore, I will bring strangers against you, the most terrible of the nations; they shall draw their swords against the beauty of your wisdom and defile your splendor. They shall thrust you down to the Pit, and you shall die a violent death in the heart of the seas. (Ezekiel 28:2, 6-8, NRSV)

BABYLONIA

Throughout history, the term "Babylonia" has been applied to different kingdoms located in southern Mesopotamia, in what is now southern Iraq. Late in the third millennium BCE, Babylonia was at different times occupied and ruled by the Sumerians and the Akkadians. Circa 1900 BCE, Babylonia was overrun by the Amorites, and the Amorites continued to

---

[125] --- (2003c)

Spreading Sin

rule until circa 1600 BCE. During this period of Amorite rule, Babylonia expanded out of southern Mesopotamia and established control over parts of Assyria in northern Mesopotamia. The foremost king of Babylonia during this period was Hammurabi (circa 1792-1750 BCE), who is famous even today for his code of laws.[126]

In 1595 BCE, Babylonia was overrun by Hittite invaders, eventually allowing Kassites from the mountains east of Babylonia to assume power over southern Mesopotamia, a rule that lasted about 400 years. It was during this period of Kassite rule that Assyria broke away from Babylonia and established its independence. Circa 1157 BCE, Elam overran the Kassites in Babylonia and established their own rule over the area. Only 30 some years later, Nebuchadrezzar I defeated Elam and ruled from circa 1124-1103 BCE. For the next few centuries after Nebuchadrezzar I, a three-way struggle developed among the Assyrians, Arameans, and Chaldeans for control of Babylonia. The Assyrians eventually won out, and they ruled over Babylonia from the ninth through the late seventh centuries BCE through a succession of puppet kings.[127]

Beginning in the late seventh century BCE, the Chaldeans established an independent Babylonia ruled by King Nabopolassar. Upon Nabopolassar's death, his son Nebuchadrezzar II ruled from 605-562 BCE. It was during this period that Babylonia established a mighty empire: northern Mesopotamia, Syria, and Palestine were conquered; the famed hanging gardens of Babylon and the Babylonian ziggurat were built; and Babylonia successfully confronted Egyptian expansion. However, despite its great might, Babylonia was overrun by the Persians under Cyrus the Great in 539 BCE. Babylonia was never again an independent kingdom, passing from the control of the Persians to that of Alexander the Great and the Macedonians in 331 BCE.[128]

---

[126] --- (2003e)
[127] --- (2003e)
[128] --- (2003e)

The First Sin: Jewish, Christian, and Islamic Perspectives

How could such a mighty empire have fallen so decisively to the Persians? According to several Biblical passages, Babylonia was defeated precisely because of its sinful pride and arrogance. For example, Isaiah 13:11 is part of a long proclamation against Babylonia that occupies the entire 13th chapter of Isaiah. Likewise, Habakkuk 2:4-5 is part of an oracle concerning Babylonia and its pride. Finally, Jeremiah 50:29-32 predicts the fall of Babylonia as God's punishment for Babylonian arrogance. In all three passages quoted immediately below, it was prophesized that God would punish and destroy the sinful pride of the arrogant Babylonian kingdom. Such punishment came in 539 BCE when Cyrus the Great and his Persian army captured the Babylonian capital of Babylon without a battle.

> I will punish the world for its evil, and the wicked for their iniquity; I will put an end to the pride of the arrogant and lay low the insolence of tyrants. (Isaiah 13:11, NRSV)

> Look at the proud! Their spirit is not right in them, but the righteous live by their faith. Moreover, wealth is treacherous; the arrogant do not endure. They open their throats wide as Sheol; like Death they never have enough. They gather all nations for themselves, and collect all peoples as their own. (Habakkuk 2:4-5, NRSV)

> Summon archers against Babylon, all who bend the bow. Encamp all around her; let no one escape. Repay her according to her deeds; just as she has done, do to her--for she has arrogantly defied the Lord, the Holy One of Israel. Therefore her young men shall fall in her squares, and all her soldiers shall be destroyed on that day, says the Lord. I am against you, O arrogant one, says the Lord God of hosts; for your day has come, the time when I will

punish you. The arrogant one shall stumble and fall, with no one to raise him up, and I will kindle a fire in his cities, and it will devour everything around him. (Jeremiah 50:29-32, NRSV)

The Edomites

According to Genesis 36:9, the Edomites were the descendants of Esau, the older twin brother of Jacob, the son of Isaac, the son of Abraham. By at least the 13th century BCE, the Edomites settled in between the Dead Sea and the Gulf of Aqaba in what is now southwestern Jordan. According to II Samuel 8:13-14 and I Kings 11:15-17, the Edomites were conquered by King David in the early 10th century BCE. Following the death of King Solomon, Edom was a vassal state under the Southern Kingdom of Judah. However, Edom successfully revolted against King Jehoram (a.k.a. Joram) of Judah in the mid-ninth century BCE and gained a brief independence before again being conquered, this time by Kings Amaziah (796-792/91 and 782/81-767 BCE) and Azariah (792/91-740/39 BCE) of Judah. They again revolted during the reign (735-716/15 BCE) of King Ahaz of the Southern Kingdom of Judah, but Edom's freedom was short-lived, as they soon became a vassal to Assyria and then later on to Babylonia. In 586 BCE, Edom allied with Babylonia in the destruction of Jerusalem and then looted a good deal of the Southern Kingdom of Judah. It was at some point after the fall of Jerusalem in 586 BCE that the Biblical book of Obadiah was written. In this Biblical book, Edom's "proud heart" is condemned, and a promise is given that Edom will be brought down. This promise was fulfilled in the fourth century BCE, when the Nabateans forced the Edomites to leave their ancestral home and migrate west into southern Judaea, where they eventually became a stateless people known as the Idumeans.[129]

---

[129] (A) Murphy RE (1971); (B) --- (2003d).

The vision of Obadiah. Thus says the Lord God concerning Edom: We have heard a report from the Lord, and a messenger has been sent among the nations: "Rise up! Let us rise against it for battle!" I will surely make you least among the nations; you shall be utterly despised. Your proud heart has deceived you, you that live in the clefts of the rock, whose dwelling is in the heights. You say in your heart, "Who will bring me down to the ground?" Though you soar aloft like the eagle, though your nest is set among the stars, from there I will bring you down, says the Lord. (Obadiah 1:1-4, NRSV)

PTOLEMAIC EGYPT

Following the death of Alexander the Great in 323 BCE, his former sprawling empire was divided up among his leading generals in 321 BCE. In the East, Seleucus I Nicator eventually assumed rule in 312 BCE. In the West, Ptolemy I Soter, the son of a Macedonian nobleman named Lagus, established himself as the ruler (satrap) of Egypt and claimed rule over Palestine in 323 BCE. He later expanded his empire to include Cyprus and Cyrene. On 11/7/305 BCE, he took the title of king. During the third century BCE, Ptolemy I Soter's successors expanded the empire to include several cities in Asia Minor, the Aegean islands, and even some towns in Thrace (the northeastern coast of modern Greece).[130]

Ptolemy I Soter died in 282 BCE, and he was succeeded by his son, Ptolemy II Philadelphus, who had become co-ruler with his father in 285 BCE and who then ruled until his death in 246 BCE. In turn, Ptolemy II Philadelphus was succeeded by Ptolemy III Euergetes, who ruled from 246 BCE until his death in 222 BCE. Euergetes was then succeeded by his son, Ptolemy IV Philopator, who ruled from 222 BCE until 205 BCE. Following Ptolemy IV Philopator, the Ptolemaic dynasty continued to rule

---

[130] Samuel AE, Bowman AK (2003).

over Egypt until falling to the Romans in 30 BCE. Egypt's last Ptolemaic ruler was Cleopatra VII, the seductress of both Julius Caesar and Mark Anthony, who died on 8/12/30 BCE.[131]

The following passage from III Maccabees centers on a specific event in the life of Ptolemy IV Philopator. While he was a weak and corrupt ruler, Ptolemy IV Philopator was also arrogant in the extreme. Following his victory over the Seleucids (see below) at Raphia in southern Palestine in 217 BCE, Ptolemy IV Philopator journeyed to Jerusalem and in his arrogance demanded to enter not only the Jewish Second Temple, but the actual Holy of Holies within the Second Temple. As the following text documents, Ptolemy IV Philopator was stricken down by God in recompense for his arrogance. (The three parenthetical insertions in the following passage were added by the current author for the sake of clarity. Of note, the "king" and the "him" that precede the parenthetical insertions are clearly identified as being "Philopator" in III Maccabees 1:1 and as being "Ptolemy" in III Maccabees 1:2 and 6. Further, Ptolemy IV Philopator's plan to enter both the Second Temple and the Holy of Holies is specifically stated in III Maccabees 1:8-15.)

> Meanwhile the crowd, as before, was engaged in prayer, while the elders near the king (Ptolemy IV Philopator) tried in various ways to change his arrogant mind from the plan that he had conceived (to enter the Jewish Second Temple and thus defile it). But he, in his arrogance, took heed of nothing, and began now to approach, determined to bring the aforesaid plan to a conclusion. When those who were around him observed this, they turned, together with our people, to call upon him who has all power to defend them in the present trouble and not to overlook this unlawful and haughty deed…Thereupon God, who oversees all things, the first

---

[131] Samuel AE, Bowman AK (2003).

Father of all, holy among the holy ones, having heard the lawful supplication, scourged him (Ptolemy IV Philopator) who had exalted himself in insolence and audacity. He shook him on this side and that as a reed is shaken by the wind, so that he lay helpless on the ground and, besides being paralyzed in his limbs, was unable even to speak, since he was smitten by a righteous judgment. Then both friends and bodyguards, seeing the severe punishment that had overtaken him, and fearing that he would lose his life, quickly dragged him out, panic-stricken in their exceedingly great fear. (III Maccabees 1:24-27; 2:21-23, NRSV)

THE SELEUCIDS

During the early years following the death of Alexander the Great in 323 BCE, as Ptolemy I Soter was carving out his Egyptian empire, one of his generals was Seleucus I Nicator (358/54-281 BCE). However, in 312 BCE, Seleucus I Nicator set out on his own and conquered what had been Babylonia. Thereafter, he expanded his empire to include Syria and Persia and ruled the Seleucid Empire until his assassination in 281 BCE at the hand of Ptolemy Ceraunus. Upon his death, he was succeeded by his son Antiochus I Soter (324-262/61 BCE), who was in turn succeeded by his son Antiochus II Theos (circa 287-246 BCE), who spent much of his reign at war with Ptolemaic Egypt. Upon his death in 246 BCE, Antiochus II Theos was succeeded by his son Seleucus II Callinicus, who ruled the Seleucid Empire until his death from a fall from his horse in 225 BCE. Seleucus II Callinicus was then succeeded by his son Seleucus III Soter, who ruled for only two years before being assassinated. Upon the death of Seleucus III Soter, he was succeeded by his younger brother, Antiochus III the Great (242-187 BCE), who was murdered in 187 BCE. Thereafter, Seleucus IV Philopator succeeded his father, Antiochus III the Great, upon his father's death and ruled until he was assassinated in 175 BCE. He was then succeeded by his brother, Antiochus IV Epiphanes (circa 215-164/63 BCE).[132]

Antiochus IV Epiphanes was king of the Seleucid Empire beginning in 175 BCE. He is described in IV Maccabees[133] 4:15 as having been "an arrogant and terrible man." In 169 BCE, Antiochus IV Epiphanes entered the Second Temple in Jerusalem and removed some of its treasures. Two years later, he: banned Jewish religious practices, including circumcision; desecrated the Second Temple by turning it into a pagan temple dedicated to Zeus and by instituting sexual debauchery and most likely the sacrifice of pigs in the Second Temple; and forced Jews to participate in the worship of the Greek god Dionysus.[134]

The extent of Antiochus IV Epiphanes' arrogance and the beginning of his punishment for his arrogance can be seen in the following two passages from II Maccabees,[135] the first of which refers to events shortly after Antiochus IV Epiphanes prohibited Jewish religious practice in 167 BCE. In this passage, it is said that Antiochus IV Epiphanes will be punished for his arrogance. The second passage quoted below appears to refer to events that took place shortly before Antiochus IV Epiphanes' death in 164/63 BCE when he was campaigning in Persia.

---

[132] (A) Seibert J (2003); (B) --- (2003g); (C) --- (2003h); (D) Varenne H (2003); (E) --- (2003i); (F) --- (2003j).

[133] IV Maccabees is usually considered to be part of the Old Testament Apocrypha. Although it is not part of the Old Testament canon of either the Roman Catholic Church or the Greek Orthodox Church, it is included as an appendix in the Greek Orthodox Bible. Dirks JF (2011). IV Maccabees was probably written originally in Greek at some point in the first century CE by a Hellenistic Jew. Anderson H (2011b).

[134] (A) Duncan GB (1971); (B) Dentan RC (1971c).

[135] II Maccabees is part of the Old Testament Apocrypha and appears in the Old Testament canon for both the Roman Catholic Church and the Greek Orthodox Church. Dirks JF (2011). II Maccabees is a condensation of a five-volume work by Jason of Cyrene. It appears to have been written early in the first century BCE, and the bulk of the work appears to have been originally written in Greek, probably in Alexandria, Egypt, by a Hellenized Jew. Dentan RC (1971c).

THE FIRST SIN: JEWISH, CHRISTIAN, AND ISLAMIC PERSPECTIVES

For our brothers after enduring a brief suffering have drunk of ever-flowing life, under God's covenant; but you, by the judgment of God, will receive just punishment for your arrogance. (II Maccabees 7:36, NRSV)

About that time, as it happened, Antiochus had retreated in disorder from the region of Persia…Transported with rage, he conceived the idea of turning upon the Jews the injury done by those who had put him to flight; so he ordered his charioteer to drive without stopping until he completed the journey. But the judgment of heaven rode with him! For in his arrogance he said, "When I get there I will make Jerusalem a cemetery of Jews." But the all-seeing Lord, the God of Israel, struck him with an incurable and invisible blow. As soon as he stopped speaking he was seized with a pain in his bowels, for which there was no relief, and with sharp internal tortures—and that very justly, for he had tortured the bowels of others with many and strange inflictions. Yet he did not in any way stop his insolence, but was even more filled with arrogance, breathing fire in his rage against the Jews, and giving orders to drive even faster. And so it came about that he fell out of his chariot as it was rushing along, and the fall was so hard as to torture every limb of his body. Thus he who only a little while before had thought in his superhuman arrogance that he could command the waves of the sea, and had imagined that he could weigh the high mountains in a balance, was brought down to earth and carried in a litter, making the power of God manifest to all. And so the ungodly man's body swarmed with worms, and while he was still living in anguish and pain, his flesh rotted away, and because of the stench the whole army felt revulsion at his decay. Because of his intolerable stench no one was able to carry the man

SPREADING SIN

who a little while before had thought that he could touch the stars of heaven. (II Maccabees 9:1, 4-10, NRSV)

The above events were not the only punishments that befell Antiochus IV Epiphanes. Of far reaching consequences for the Seleucid Empire, Antiochus IV Epiphanes' arrogant prohibition of the Jewish religion and his desecration of the Second Temple resulted in Jewish revolt under Judas Maccabeus, which began in 166 BCE. Two years later, in 164 BCE, while Antiochus IV Epiphanes was fighting a campaign in Persia, Judas Maccabeus and his Jewish guerilla forces captured Jerusalem and rededicated the Second Temple to the Jewish religion. Shortly thereafter, King Antiochus IV Epiphanes died in Tabae, Iran, in 164/63 BCE.

Antiochus IV Epiphanes was succeeded upon his death in 164/63 BCE by Antiochus V Eupator, who ruled for only a brief period before Demetrius I Soter, the son of Seleucus IV Philopator, seized the Seleucid throne in 162 BCE. Demetrius I Soter then ruled until his death in 150 BCE.[136]

It was while the Seleucid Empire was under the rule of Demetrius I Soter that the Seleucid general Nicanor, the commander of the Syrian elephant corps, was sent to retake Palestine from the Maccabean revolutionaries. Nicanor was a proud and arrogant man who vowed to burn down the Second Temple if Judas Maccabeus and his guerilla army did not surrender to him. However, as the following verses from I Maccabees illustrate, Nicanor's arrogance was punished by God through the use of Judas Maccabeus and his army in 161 BCE.[137] Nicanor was defeated, and his army was completely routed. Nicanor was killed in the fighting, and his amputated head was later displayed as a trophy near Jerusalem.

After these events Nicanor went up to Mount Zion. Some of the

---

[136] (A) --- (2003k); (B) Duncan GB (1971).
[137] Flusser D (2003).

priests from the sanctuary and some of the elders of the people came out to greet him peaceably and to show him the burnt offering that was being offered for the king. But he mocked them and derided them and defiled them and spoke arrogantly, and in anger he swore this oath, "Unless Judas and his army are delivered into my hands this time, then if I return safely I will burn up this house."...Now Nicanor went out from Jerusalem and encamped in Beth-horon, and the Syrian army joined him. Judas encamped in Adasa with three thousand men...So the armies met in battle on the thirteenth day of the month of Adar. The army of Nicanor was crushed, and he himself was the first to fall in the battle. When his army saw that Nicanor had fallen, they threw down their arms and fled. The Jews pursued them a day's journey, from Adasa as far as Gazara, and as they followed they kept sounding the battle call on the trumpets. People came out of all the surrounding villages of Judea, and they outflanked the enemy and drove them back to their pursuers, so that they all fell by the sword; not even one of them was left. Then the Jews seized the spoils and the plunder; they cut off Nicanor's head and the right hand that he had so arrogantly stretched out, and brought them and displayed them just outside Jerusalem. (I Maccabees 7:33-35, 39-40, 43-47, NRSV)

The Maccabean revolution continued after the aforementioned battle between Judas Maccabeus and the Seleucid Empire. Upon being killed in battle in 160 BCE, Judas Maccabeus was succeeded in command of the Jewish revolutionaries by his brother Jonathon. When Jonathon was murdered in 143 BCE, his brother Simon became the leader of the Jewish independence movement. Finally, in 142 BCE, the Jewish revolutionaries in Palestine were able to gain their independence from the

Seleucid Empire.[138]

POLYTHEISTS OF MAKKAH

By the sixth century CE, Makkah had become an important caravan stop between Syria to the north and Yemen to the south. It had also become an important pilgrimage center where numerous different Arab tribes housed their idols and religious relics in the Ka'ba, the more or less cube-shaped building that stood in the center of Makkah. Fueled by both caravans and pilgrimages, the polytheists of Makkah had become both influential across the western Arabian Peninsula and reasonably wealthy.

Given that part of Makkah's wealth and prestige came from the idolatrous pilgrims that journeyed to the Ka'ba, the polytheists of Makkah were eager to stop the monotheistic preaching of Prophet Muhammad, which they saw as being both antithetical to their own religious beliefs and a threat to their influence and economic wellbeing. As such, in their arrogance, they persecuted Prophet Muhammad and the early Muslim community. However, their arrogance resulted in a God-given famine that afflicted the whole of Makkah.

> If We were merciful to (the idol-worshippers of Mecca) and relieved them of the agonizing (famine) from which they've been suffering, then they would still eagerly persist in their rebelliousness, wandering all around in distraction.
>
> We punished them with this (famine so they could learn a lesson), but they've neither humbled themselves before their Lord, nor have they begged Him (for relief). (Their arrogance will continue)—even until We open a door for them that will lead to a painful punishment. Then they'll be in abject despair within (their place of doom)! (*Qur'an* 23:75-77, Emerick translation)

---
[138] Duncan GB (1971).

As the above Qur'anic passage indicates, the arrogance of the Makkan polytheists continued despite the famine that punished them. Their persecution of the early Muslims continued and eventually contributed to Prophet Muhammad and the Muslim community migrating from Makkah to Madinah in 622 CE. Finally, in 630 CE, God bestowed victory upon the Muslims and punished the polytheists of Makkah when the Muslim community of Madinah captured Makkah in what was an almost totally bloodless conquest. The polytheist community of Makkah basically surrendered without a fight, and most Makkans finally converted to Islam. The following Qur'anic passage foretells the fall of polytheistic Makkah when it states that: "They were arrogant in the earth and plotted evil, but evil plots only trap those who weave them!"

> The (idol-worshippers) swore their most sacred oaths that if a warner ever came to them, they would follow his guidance even better than any other nation, but when a warner did come to them, it only made them run away that much faster! They were arrogant in the earth and plotted evil, but evil plots only trap those who weave them! Are they waiting for the fate that ancient (civilizations) suffered? You'll never find any change in God's methods, nor will you ever find any other way except God's way. (*Qur'an* 35:42-43, Emerick translation)

CONCLUSIONS

All of the above mentioned leaders and kingdoms are said to have been humbled, if not altogether destroyed, because of their arrogance and self-pride. Some were punished or annihilated by what appear to be events that can be explained by natural events, although natural events that were commanded by God. This would be the case with the people of Noah, the 'Ad, the Thamud, the Midianites, and King Jeroboam and King

Spreading Sin

Azariah of the Northern Kingdom of Israel, who were variously afflicted with floods, earthquakes, and leprosy. Other leaders and kingdoms were afflicted with punishments that appear more supernatural in character. This would be the case with the fire and sulfur that fell from Heaven on Sodom and Gomorrah, the Egyptian army that was pursuing Moses and the Israelites and that was drowned in a sea that had miraculously parted and then closed, Korah who was sucked down into the earth, the army of King Sennacherib of Assyria being slain by an angel, and Ptolemy IV Philopator's strange bodily affliction. Still other leaders and countries were stricken down by other peoples. This would be the case with the final fall of the Northern Kingdom of Israel, King Sennacherib of Assyria being assassinated, the final defeat of Assyria, Pharaoh Hophra, King Hezekiah of the Southern Kingdom of Judah, King Amon of the Southern Kingdom of Judah being assassinated, King Zedekiah and the final fall of the Southern Kingdom of Judah, Moab, Tyre, Babylonia, Edom, the Seleucids, and the polytheists of Makkah. This latter mode of God's punishment for national arrogance, i.e., having one people or country destroying another, is directly mentioned in the *Qur'an*.

> If God didn't use one set of people to check (the ambitions) of another, then there would've been many monasteries, churches, synagogues and mosques, which are used to commemorate the name of God abundantly, pulled down and ruined. (*Qur'an* 22:40, Emerick translation)

In closing, it should be noted that the events described above are not merely stories from the pages of a distant history. They are also warnings for present and future leaders and countries. National arrogance is despised by God, and arrogant nations will eventually be brought down to their knees, if not actually destroyed.

THE FIRST SIN: JEWISH, CHRISTIAN, AND ISLAMIC PERSPECTIVES

When one country meddles in the affairs of another, is it out of genuine humanitarian concerns, or is it a reflection of a national arrogance, a belief that one's own country's rules, customs, and form of government are necessarily superior to that of another? It is a fine line between humanitarian intervention and national arrogance. While humanitarian concerns can properly lead a humble country to intervene in the affairs of another in order to stop genocide, a flagrant disregard for human rights, etc., the motive must be pure. One can only hope and pray that it is not pride and arrogance that lead one country to intervene in or seek to control another, for that is the path to destruction. That should be a warning to all countries of the current age, especially for the so-called super powers.

Does this warning mean that one country should never economically or militarily intervene in the affairs of another country? No, it most certainly does not. There are times and situations that cry out for such intervention. World War II offers a case in point. The Nazi atrocities against Jews, Gypsies, Slavs, the mentally impaired, and the physically deformed, as well as the Japanese military's barbarisms in Korea and Manchuria, demanded outside military intervention. Indeed, with regard to such military intervention, the *Qur'an* specifically states that military intervention is warranted to relieve the suffering of an oppressed people.

> And why shouldn't you fight in the cause of God and in the cause of those who, being weak, are mistreated: the men, women and children whose only cry is, "Our Lord! Deliver us from this land whose people are oppressors. Send us someone from You who will protect us, and send us someone from You who will help!" (*Qur'an* 4:75)

There is at times justification in intervening militarily or economically in the affairs of another country. However, when we look at world events over the last several decades, we find American military intervention, whether by boots on the ground or planes in the air, in Lebanon, Granada, Panama, the former Yugoslavia, Somalia, Iraq, Afghanistan, Libya, Yemen, and Pakistan. In addition, how many countries have felt the impact of American economic pressure and sanctions? Are all these interventions the result of a pure and untainted motive to help the unfairly oppressed, or can each such intervention be solely justified on the grounds of national self-defense? Has the American military become the world's policeman only out of humanitarian concerns, or is it out of some measure of hubris and national arrogance? Having intervened, whether militarily or economically, do we allow the other country to form its own identity and way, or do we arrogantly pressure the other country to adopt our customs and ways of government?

As noted previously, when one intervenes in the affairs of another country, there is a fine line between humanitarian concerns and national arrogance. This author does not presume to know exactly where that line is; the world is far too complicated for that. However, this author has the right, as do all Americans and all people of faith, to raise the question as to where that line is and to whether or not we are crossing over that line, a line that separates humanitarian concerns from a national arrogance that can only lead to our own self-destruction.

Bibliography

Abu Dawud (Al-Azdi SA): *Kitab Al-Sunan.* In Hasan A (trans.): *Sunan Abu Dawud.* New Delhi, Kitab Bhavan, 1990.

Ackroyd PR: The Book of Isaiah. In Laymon CM (ed.): *The Interpreter's One-Volume Commentary on the Bible.* Nashville, Abingdon Press, 1971.

Ad-Din W: *Mishkat Al-Masabih.* In Robson J (trans.): *Mishkat Al-Masabih.* Lahore, Sh. Muhammad Ashraf, 1963.

Albeck H (ed.): *Midrash Bereshit Rabbati.* Jerusalem, Mekize Nirdamim, 1940.

Al-Bukhari MI: *Kitab Al-Jami' Al-Sahih.* In Khan MM (trans): *The Translation of the Meanings of Sahih Al-Bukhari.* Madinah, ---, undated.

Al-Tabari M: *Ta'rikh Al-Rusul Wa'l-Muluk.* In Rosenthal F (trans.): *The History of Al-Tabari: Volume One—General Introduction and from the Creation to the Flood.* Albany, State University of New York Press, 1989.

Al-Tabari M: *Ta'rikh Al-Rusul Wa'l-Muluk.* In Brinner WM (trans.): *The History of Al-Tabari: Volume Two—Prophets and Patriarchs.* Albany, State University of New York Press, 1987.

Al-Tirmidhi MI: *Al-Jami' Al-Sahih.* In --- (trans.): *Sahih Al-Tirmidhi.* In --- (eds.): *Alim Multimedia CD Rom.* ---, ISL Software Corporation, ---.

Algar H: Refusing to bow to Adam. In --- (eds.): *Encyclopaedia Iranica.* www.iranian.com, 1997.

'Ali 'AY: *The Meaning of the Holy Qur'an* (11th Edition). Beltsville, amana publications, 2009.

Andersen FI: 2 (Slavonic Apocalypse of) Enoch. In Charlesworth JH (ed.): *The Old Testament Pseudepigrapha: Volume One.* Peabody, Hendrickson Publishers, 2011.

Anderson H: 3 Maccabees. In Charlesworth JH (ed.): *The Old Testament Pseudepigrapha: Volume One.* Peabody, Hendrickson Publishers, 2011a.

Anderson H: 4 Maccabees. In Charlesworth JH (ed.): *The Old Testament Pseudepigrapha: Volume One.* Peabody, Hendrickson Publishers, 2011b.

An-Nawawi Y: *Riyad Us-Saliheen.* In Matraji M (trans.): *Riyad Us-Saliheen.* Beirut, Dar El-Fiker, 1993.

Beavin EL: Ecclesiasticus or the Wisdom of Jesus the son of Sirach. In Laymon CM (ed.): *The Interpreter's One-Volume Commentary on the Bible.* Nashville, Abingdon Press, 1971.

BIBLIOGRAPHY

Bercot D: *A Dictionary of Early Christian Beliefs*. Peabody, Hendrickson Publishers, 1998.

Brownlee WH: The Book of Ezekiel. In Laymon CM (ed.): *The Interpreter's One-Volume Commentary on the Bible*. Nashville, Abingdon Press, 1971.

Carstensen RN: The Book of Zechariah. In Laymon CM (ed.): *The Interpreter's One-Volume Commentary on the Bible*. Nashville, Abingdon Press, 1971.

Clapp N: *The Road to Ubar—Finding the Atlantis of the Sands*. Boston, Houghton Mifflin Company, 1998.

Cowley AE: Judith. In Charles RH (ed.): *The Apocrypha and Pseudepigrapha of the Old Testament in English: Volume I: Apocrypha*. Oxford, Clarendon Press, 1971.

Crapps RW: Image of God. In Mills WE (ed.): *Mercer Dictionary of the Bible*. Macon, Mercer University Press, 1997.

Dentan RC: The Second Book of Esdras. In Laymon CM (ed.): *The Interpreter's One-Volume Commentary on the Bible*. Nashville, Abingdon Press, 1971a.

Dentan RC: The Wisdom of Solomon. In Laymon CM (ed.): *The Interpreter's One-Volume Commentary on the Bible*. Nashville, Abingdon Press, 1971b.

Dentan RC: The Second Book of the Maccabees. In Laymon CM (ed.): *The Interpreter's One-Volume Commentary on the Bible.* Nashville, Abingdon Press, 1971c.

Dirks JF: Abraham: *The Friend of God.* Beltsville, amana publications, 2002.

Dirks JF: *Understanding Islam: A Guide for the Judaeo-Christian Reader.* Beltsville, amana publications, 2003.

Dirks JF: *The Abrahamic Faiths: Judaism, Christianity, and Islam: Similarities and Contrasts.* Beltsville, amana publications, 2004.

Dirks JF: *Letters to My Elders in Islam.* Beltsville, amana publications, 2008.

Dirks JF: *What You Weren't Taught in Sunday School.* Beltsville, amana publications, 2011.

Dowd SE: Maccabees, Third. In Mills WE (ed.): *Mercer Dictionary of the Bible.* Macon, Mercer University Press, 1997.

Duncan GB: Chronology. In Laymon CM (ed.): *The Interpreter's One-Volume Commentary on the Bible.* Nashville, Abingdon Press, 1971.

Durand VM, Barlow DH: *Essentials of Abnormal Psychology: Fourth Edition.* ---, Thomson Wadsworth, 2006.

BIBLIOGRAPHY

Emerick Y: *The Meaning of the Holy Qur'an in Today's English— Extended Study Edition.* New York, IFNA, 2000.

Emerick Y: *A Journey through the Holy Qur'an.* New York, IFNA, 2009.

Emmet CW: The Third Book of Maccabees. In Charles RH (ed.): *The Apocrypha and Pseudepigrapha of the Old Testament in English: Volume I:* Apocrypha. Oxford, University Press, 1971.

Flusser D: Biblical Literature: Intertestamental literature. In --- (ed.): *Encyclopaedia Britannica 2003.* ---, Encyclopaedia Britannica, 2003.

Hyatt JP: The Compiling of Israel's Story. In Laymon CM (ed.): *The Interpreter's One-Volume Commentary on the Bible.* Nashville, Abingdon Press, 1971.

Ibn Kathir I: *Tafsir Al-Qur'an Al-'Azim.* In Shagif A, Al-Mubarakpuri S, et al. (eds.): *Al-Misbah Al-Munir Fi Tahdhib Tafsir Ibn Kathir.* In Abualrub J, Khitab N, Khitab H, Walker A, Al-Jibali M, Ayoub S (trans.): *Tafsir Ibn Kathir (Abridged).* Riyadh, Darussalam, 2000.

Isaac E: I (Ethiopic Apocalypse of) Enoch. In Charlesworth JH (ed.): *The Old Testament Pseudepigrapha: Volume One.* Peabody, Hendrickson Publishers, 2011.

Jacobs J, Blau L: Satan. In --- (eds.): *Jewish Encyclopedia.* www.jewishencyclopedia.com.

Johnson MD: Life of Adam and Eve. In Charlesworth JH (ed.):
The Old Testament Pseudepigrapha: Volume Two.
Peabody, Hendrickson Publishers, 2011.

Kee HC: Testaments of the Twelve Patriarchs. In Charlesworth JH (ed.):
The Old Testament Pseudepigrapha: Volume One.
Peabody, Hendrickson Publishers, 2011.

Knibb MA: Martyrdom and Ascension of Isaiah. In Charlesworth JH (ed.):
The Old Testament Pseudepigrapha: Volume Two.
Peabody, Hendrickson Publishers, 2011.

Knight GAF: The First Book of the Maccabees. In Laymon CM (ed.):
The Interpreter's One-Volume Commentary on the Bible.
Nashville, Abingdon Press, 1971.

Kuemmerlin-McLean J: Satan in the Old Testament. In Mills WE (ed.):
Mercer Dictionary of the Bible. Macon, Mercer University Press, 1997.

Malik (Al-Asbahi M): *Al-Muwatta.* In Rahimuddin M (trans.):
Muwatta Imam Malik. Lahore, Sh. Muhammad Ashraf, 1985.

Millon T: *Disorders of Personality—DSM III: Axis III.* New York, John Wiley & Sons, 1981.

Murphy RE: The Book of Obadiah. In Laymon CM (ed.):
The Interpreter's One-Volume Commentary on the Bible.
Nashville, Abingdon Press, 1971.

Muslim (Al-Qushayri MH): *Al-Jami' Al-Sahih.* In Siddiqi 'AH (trans.): *Sahih Muslim.* ---, ---, 1971.

Neusner J: *The Babylonian Talmud—A Translation and Commentary on CD-Rom.* ---, Hendrickson Publishers, 2005.

Oesterley WOE: I Maccabees. In Charles RH (ed.): *The Apocrypha and Pseudepigrapha of the Old Testament in English: Volume I: Apocrypha.* Oxford, Clarendon Press, 1971.

Olson MJ: Angel. In Mills WE (ed.): *Mercer Dictionary of the Bible.* Macon, Mercer University Press, 1997.

Peacock HF: Tobit, Book of. In Mills WE (ed.): *Mercer Dictionary of the Bible.* Macon, Mercer University Press, 1997a.

Peacock HF: Solomon, Wisdom of. In Mills WE (ed.): *Mercer Dictionary of the Bible.* Macon, Mercer University Press, 1997b.

Richardson HN: The Book of Tobit. In Laymon CM (ed.): *The Interpreter's One-Volume Commentary on the Bible.* Nashville, Abingdon Press, 1971a.

Richardson HN: The Book of Judith. In Laymon CM (ed.): *The Interpreter's One-Volume Commentary on the Bible.* Nashville, Abingdon Press, 1971b.

Rutledge DW: Satan in the New Testament. In Mills WE (ed.): *Mercer Dictionary of the Bible.* Macon, Mercer University Press, 1997.

Samuel AE, Bowman AK: Egypt: History: Macedonian and Ptolemaic Egypt (332-30 BCE). In --- (ed.): *Encyclopaedia Britannica 2003.* ---, Encyclopaedia Britannica, 2003.

Seibert J: Seleucus I Nicator. In --- (ed.): *Encyclopaedia Britannica 2003.* ---, Encyclopaedia Britannica, 2003.

Simpson DC: Tobit. In Charles RH: *The Apocrypha and Pseudepigrapha of the Old Testament in English: Volume I: Apocrypha.* Oxford, Oxford University Press, 1971.

Smith W: *A Dictionary of the Bible.* Elgin, Brethren Publishing House, ---.

Sweet LM: Satan. In --- (ed.): *International Standard Bible Encyclopedia.* In --- (eds.): *Ellis Maxima Bible Library.* Oklahoma City, Ellis Enterprises, Inc., 2001.

Usmani SA: *Tafsir.* In Ahmad MA (trans.): *The Noble Qur'an— Tafseer-'E-Usmani.* New Delhi, Idrara Isha'at-E-Diniyat (P) Ltd., 1992.

Varenne H: Antiochus III. In --- (ed.): *Encyclopaedia Britannica 2003.* ---, Encyclopaedia Britannica, 2003.

Vinson RB: Baal-zebub/Baal-zebul. In Mills WE (ed.): *Mercer Dictionary of the Bible.* Macon, Mercer University Press, 1997.

Wintermute OS: Jubilees. In Charlesworth JH (ed.):
The Old Testament Pseudepigrapha: Volume Two.
Peabody, Hendrickson Publishers, 2011.

---: *Diagnostic and Statistical Manual of Mental Disorders: Fourth Edition.*
Washington, American Psychiatric Association, 1994.

---: Assyria. In --- (ed.): *Encyclopaedia Britannica 2003.* ---,
Encyclopaedia Britannica, 2003a.

---: Moabite. In --- (ed.): *Encyclopaedia Britannica 2003.* ---,
Encyclopaedia Britannica, 2003b.

---: Tyre. In --- (ed.): *Encyclopaedia Britannica 2003.* ---,
Encyclopaedia Britannica, 2003c.

---: Edom. In --- (ed.): *Encyclopaedia Britannica 2003.* ---,
Encyclopaedia Britannica, 2003d.

---: Babylonia. In --- (ed.): *Encyclopaedia Britannica* 2003. ---,
Encyclopaedia Britannica, 2003e.

---: Philistine. In --- (ed.): *Encyclopaedia Britannica* 2003. ---,
Encyclopaedia Britannica, 2003f.

---: Antiochus II Theos. In --- (ed.): *Encyclopaedia Britannica 2003.* ---,
Encyclopaedia Britannica, 2003g.

---: Seleucus II Callinicus. In --- (ed.): *Encyclopaedia Britannica 2003*.
---, Encyclopaedia Britannica, 2003h.

---: Seleucus III, Soter. In --- (ed.): *Encyclopaedia Britannica 2003*.
---, Encyclopaedia Britannica, 2003i.

---: Seleucus IV Philopator. In --- (ed.): *Encyclopaedia Britannica 2003*.
---, Encyclopaedia Britannica, 2003j.

---: Demetrius I Soter. In --- (ed.): *Encyclopaedia Britannica 2003*.
---, Encyclopaedia Britannica, 2003k.

OTHER BOOKS
AUTHORED BY DR. JERALD F. DIRKS
AND PUBLISHED BY AMANA PUBLICATIONS

The Cross and the Crescent

Abraham, The Friend of God

Understanding Islam: A Guide for the Judaeo-Christian Reader

The Abrahamic Faiths: Judaism, Christianity, and Islam

Muslims in American History: A Forgotten Legacy

Letters to my Elders in Islam

What You Weren't Taught in Sunday School